Parents in my podcast community repeatedly ask for my support in merging their families' faith with their local public schools. Kori Pennypacker's *Backpack Faith* is the perfect answer. Every public-school parent should read this book! With powerful energy, Kori dispels common myths and misconceptions about public schools while equipping, inspiring, and empowering your family to live out your faith daily!

COURTNEY DEFEO, host of the *Pardon the Mess* podcast

Backpack Faith is filled with abundant tools to help parents ensure that their children are emotionally and spiritually equipped to live out their faith in an increasingly secular society. Having fought in court for First Amendment protections, I know how indispensable freedom of speech and religious liberty are to our nation's students. Kori Pennypacker brings context and clarity through personal stories, real-life application, and compassionate models of engagement that are grounded in biblical truth. Every Christian parent needs *Backpack Faith* to empower him or her to impact public education with Christlike courage.

RYAN BOMBERGER, cofounder of the Radiance Foundation and former participant in Bible2School

Parents, you will definitely want a copy of *Backpack Faith* in your hands as the school year begins. This valuable tool will give your family confidence, wisdom, and peace to live out your faith no matter where your child goes to school. And you will love the stories of how God is moving on our school campuses! At Moms in Prayer International, we are so grateful to Kori and the Bible2School ministry for bringing God's truth to children in public schools.

SALLY BURKE, president of Moms in Prayer International (momsinprayer.org)

Kori Pennypacker's *Backpack Faith* grabs you from the start, helping you understand the realities your kids face and the rights they have while living out their faith in public school. While sharing her family's experiences, Kori clarifies policies, explains the law, and gives tested tips for the journey. You'll love her relentless energy as she presents truth and helps families live for God.

Jerry Pattengale, PhD, senior adviser and founding scholar of the Museum of the Bible

As a mom of two boys in public school, I felt inspired and challenged by the eye-opening truths in *Backpack Faith*. Kori Pennypacker shares her experience and wisdom in a way that makes complex topics accessible and easy to understand. I am already applying the practical tools to pray for and encourage my sons to live out their faith with confidence! This is a must-read guide for anyone raising children to love the Lord and boldly live their lives for Him.

Sara Murphy, vice president of brand strategy at Sight & Sound Theatres

Backpack Faith

FOCUS ON THE FAMILY®

A Focus on the Family resource published by
Tyndale House Publishers

Helping Your Child Live Confidently for Jesus in Public School
BACKPACK FAITH
Jesus
JESUS
HOLY
KORI PENNYPACKER

A Focus on the Family book published by Tyndale House Publishers, Carol Stream, Illinois 60188

Cover design by Eunseo Ko

Interior design by Cathy Miller

People's names and certain details of their stories have been changed to protect the privacy of the individuals involved. However, the facts of what happened and the underlying principles have been conveyed as accurately as possible.

For information about special discounts for bulk purchases, please contact Tyndale House Publishers at csresponse@tyndale.com, or call 1-855-277-9400.

ISBN 978-1-64607-221-7

Printed in the United States of America

32 31 30 29 28 27 26
7 6 5 4 3 2 1

To Jesus, my Lord and my God and my foundation for life.

To my husband, Blaine, who led me to Jesus and continues to give me his steady, gentle, loving support in all our adventures with the perfect measure of laughter.

To my sons, Justin, Matthew, and Benjamin, and their beautiful wives, who continually shower me with grace, love, and hugs on this lifelong parenting journey.

CONTENTS

Foreword by Alex Kendrick xi

INTRODUCTION The Power of Confident Faith 1

PART ONE **KNOWING YOUR ROLE AND THE RULES**

CHAPTER 1 You're the Starter 7

CHAPTER 2 Understanding the Rules of the Game 23

PART TWO **THREE WAYS CHILDREN CAN FREELY EXPRESS THEIR FAITH AT SCHOOL**

CHAPTER 3 Expressing Faith Individually 41

CHAPTER 4 Expressing Faith with Others 55

CHAPTER 5 Expressing Faith in Class and at School Events 69

PART THREE **UNIQUE SPACES FOR THE BIBLE IN PUBLIC SCHOOL**

CHAPTER 6 How the Bible Can Transform Kids' Lives 87

CHAPTER 7 Before- and After-School Bible Clubs 101

CHAPTER 8 Bible-Literacy Classes 115

CHAPTER 9 Released-Time Bible Programs 129

PART FOUR **PREPARING YOUR KIDS TO GET IN THE GAME**

CHAPTER 10 Preparing Versus Protecting 143

CHAPTER 11 Playing on the Same Team 159

CHAPTER 12 Kindly Educating the Educators 173

CHAPTER 13 Conversation Tools for Kids 187

CHAPTER 14 Role Models on Speed Dial 207

CHAPTER 15 It's Time to Get in the Game! 223

Acknowledgments 233

APPENDIX *Backpack Faith* Resources 237

Notes 241

About the Author 251

FOREWORD

I was startled! I sat there as a college freshman in a class of about sixty students while my biology professor rolled her eyes when I admitted to being a Christian. She said out loud, "There's always one." She refused to acknowledge anything other than evolution and urged us not to express any religious views in her classroom.

How do I respond to that? Do I just keep my mouth shut? How should I live out my faith in a public school?

I'll admit that at the time I didn't know the legal rights and freedoms that are afforded to students. So my confidence was low as I tried to process the appropriate way to live out my faith. And honestly, that's where many parents are today as they try to determine how to guide their children as they walk into public schools.

That's why the book you're reading is so needed and powerful. It will help you look at your priceless children and their education from a biblical perspective (along with a needed legal perspective).

I first met Kori Pennypacker in 2021, when I was introduced to released-time Bible programs and the laws that supported and allowed the Bible to be shared and taught in public-school settings. I kept asking myself, *How did I not know about this?* as she walked me through their Bible2School organization. It was an eye-opening experience to see how many opportunities we have to share the gospel of Jesus Christ with thousands of public-school students in a loving and nurturing way and with the legal support of our Supreme Court and American laws.

Here's the bottom line: When you know your role and know the rules, you can move forward effectively and fruitfully. That's how ball teams win games and businesses grow. That's how relationships bloom and ministries expand. And that's how you and your children can confidently engage in conversations and programs in your local public schools that inspire others and share the beautiful light of our faith.

As you read this book, you will have dozens of questions answered about how to fruitfully interact with your schoolteachers and administrators along with how to help your own children live out their faith among their friends and classmates. Your mindset will grow beyond just protecting your sons and daughters to preparing them for school interactions and conversations regarding their faith, because most teachers and administrators aren't even fully aware of what the law says.

I encourage you to start with prayer and then make time to read this book from cover to cover. You'll be challenged and inspired while also getting the game plan for your family and children to make a difference in your educational arena. The Lord is raising up a generation who walks with Him and shares Him with others in a powerful way, so we invite you to jump in! You'll be glad you did.

Get ready to be salt and light, and may God richly bless you as you soak up these pages!

Alex Kendrick
pastor and filmmaker (*War Room*, *Fireproof*)

INTRODUCTION

THE POWER OF CONFIDENT FAITH

Has God been removed from public schools? We hear that message a lot. Perhaps it isn't so much that God has been taken out of schools as that many Christians have left Him at the front door.

Yes, it's true that public schools have become increasingly hostile to Christian beliefs. But no authority on earth has the power to keep God from being anyplace He wants to be. It's time for Christian parents to confront the misconceptions about the "separation of church and state." God is calling us to help our children confidently carry their faith with them as they face challenges at school and in life.

As a former public-school mom, I wrote this book to encourage and equip Christian parents who are asking the question I hear most often: "Can my children confidently live out their faith in a public school?" Lack of clarity is causing parents and children to respond with fear, complacency, and avoidance. We must quiet the fear to bring the truth to light. Our kids' spiritual development depends on it. Children *can* confidently bring their faith into the public school—and respectfully share and defend it.

Courage and confidence require preparation. This takes time

and a concerted effort on the part of parents, but the rewards of diligently training children to turn to the Lord in all matters, including education, will reap lifelong benefits.

I've heard many stories of children boldly reflecting God's love and truth in public schools, even when adults cower. Let me share one of those stories from Anna, an elementary school teacher:

> Fear crackled through the classroom as twenty-five of my third-grade students crouched on their hands and knees against their lockers along the wall, out of sight of the hallway. They'd practiced active-shooter drills many times, but as far as we knew, this wasn't a drill. We thought there was a dangerous intruder in our building. Several girls cried and hiccupped to catch their breath. There was a wave of whispering as they hugged each other.
>
> "I am so scared."
>
> "Me too."
>
> My mind raced. *How do I keep my kids safe?* The principal's voice boomed instructions over the loudspeaker. "Lock the windows. Close the blinds." I was on the edge of panic and couldn't think clearly.
>
> Then I looked up and saw a small group of children huddled together and praying aloud to God for the safety of our class and our school. In an instant, their faith encouraged me. I was reminded that Jesus never leaves us. That moment of clarity helped me get myself together to comfort and lead my students.
>
> This group of children had been attending a new Bible program that came to our school last year, and their lives have not been the same since. Although this intruder

alert thankfully ended up being a false alarm, the faithful example of these precious praying children led me to the God they knew was with them. To Him be the glory!

Facing darkness, these third-grade children let the light of their faith shine brightly in a dangerous situation. They prayed for the safety of their classmates and everyone else in the school. These children radiated confidence and peace, helping their frightened teacher recognize that God is always near. Their actions inspired her to stay calm and care for her students. She saw God working through her students as they lived out their faith in a public-school setting.

I think most parents want their children to have this confidence and peace of mind. Whether you're concerned about school curriculum, peer pressure, or the persecution of your child's faith, I pray this book will equip and empower you to embrace your role in discipling and preparing your children to live out their faith.

If you would like your child's faith to grow and flourish in a public-school setting, read on. This book is filled with stories of children whose faith thrived in public school, truths about expressing faith at school, ideas for equipping your child, and ways to graciously respond when your family's freedoms are violated. We'll also fill your child's backpack with the supplies they need to thrive. And when we're done, you'll feel much more equipped, inspired, and confident to act.

Can your children confidently live out their faith in public school?

Yes, they can!

And I can't wait to show you how.

PART ONE

Knowing Your Role and the Rules

CHAPTER 1

YOU'RE THE STARTER

"Where is he? Do you see number 3?"

My husband and I scanned the grassy field lined with chalk-white numbers, lines, and dashes, and now dotted with little red-and-blue helmets. Craning our necks to see around the heads of other eager parents looking for their sons, we were excited for our son's debut on the opening day of youth-football season. We had been waiting for this day for a long time. The blinding sun bounced off the shiny metal bleachers into our eyes, making the task of locating our son's red jersey nearly impossible. One interesting thing about the first day of football season with young elementary schoolers is that you are never quite prepared for how small the kids are or how different they look with their full pads and helmets on—puffed up and almost unrecognizable. We laughed to ourselves, as some players were nearly as wide as they were tall, wobbling across the field under all the padding. *How do they stay upright?*

We finally spotted our boy standing on the sidelines in a huddle of players listening to the coach's instructions. The kickoff and the first play got underway, and our son stayed on the sidelines. Then the second play, the third, and the fourth progressed—still, number 3 didn't trot onto the field. We were a bit confused. Our son had been proud that he had been picked as a starter for his position, but he remained on the sidelines. What was happening down there?

My husband and I tried to guess what was going on. Maybe the coach was upset with our kid. Or maybe our son hadn't understood the coach's expectations and instructions. Did our son not understand some rules? Was he intimidated by the other players?

On the car ride home, we asked him why he hadn't taken the field for a single play in his long-awaited, first-ever youth-football game. He had been so excited. With wide, innocent eyes, he explained to us that he would have played, but every time he was ready to run onto the field, another player who shared his position told him loudly and confidently, "You stay here. It's my turn!"

CHEERING FROM THE BLEACHERS

Like my husband and I at our son's football game, many Christian parents find themselves watching their children's faith journeys from the bleachers and wondering why their kids aren't in the game. Confronted with the staggering statistics of kids abandoning the Christian faith,[1] everyone is looking for answers, searching for sure footing in an unstable world. Parents are concerned not only about the changing culture but also about how it is influencing the education of their children.

According to a yearly Gallup poll, as of 2024, almost 80 percent of Christian parents in our nation chose to send their children to public school.[2] The reasons for choosing public schools vary as much as the families themselves. While many might want a private Christian education for their kids, the cost is often prohibitive. Others reason, "I went to public school and turned out okay. Won't they?"

Whatever their reasons, many Christian parents don't know how to equip their kids to live out their faith in public school. Much like my son in his first game of youth football, parents and kids are often confused, timid, and fearful that their faith will be consumed by an education system they feel powerless to control and don't fully understand.

When it comes to our kids living out their faith, we don't just want them to get in the game; we want them to flourish. Jesus is not only "the way, and the truth, and the life" (John 14:6); He is the foundation for life itself.

If you're holding this book in your hands, you are likely already certain what you would like the outcome of your child's faith to be: a dynamic relationship with the Lord. You want your child to grow into a young adult who will not only stand courageously for Jesus but will also share Him confidently with peers.

For years, I have walked alongside parents and students living out their faith in a public-school environment. Here are just a few of the questions they've asked on this journey:

- "Can my children walk through the doors of a public school without having their faith destroyed?"
- "What can I do if my children's faith and freedoms are violated?"
- "Are my kids being stifled at school if they want to talk about their faith?"

- "Do my children have the freedom to read their Bibles in school? Can they pray?"
- "Exactly what can and can't my kids do when it comes to expressing their faith in a public school?"
- "What can and can't public-school teachers do about kids expressing their faith?"

To complicate matters, the rules and expectations for expressing religious beliefs in public schools have become increasingly unclear. Not only is it unclear to students and parents, but unfortunately, many misinformed teachers and administrators often overstep the rules when it comes to students' religious or speech rights. When facts aren't clear, the loudest or most confident voices rule the day. But the loudest and most politically or culturally correct answers aren't always true.

Kids are often told to check their faith at the front door of public school. But if they can express their faith at home, why should it be any different at school? Is there some law that forbids this? Did our Founding Fathers really say that our kids can't express their spiritual side in our public schools? Why would we ever ask our kids to leave such an important part of themselves at home?

Sadly, without answers to these questions, many Christian parents continue watching from the bleachers while their kids stand on the sidelines and never get in the game. A potentially bold witness remains a light hidden under a basket, and our kids' faith development suffers because of it. Some kids even wander from their faith because a pattern has been established that keeps their spiritual lives separate from their school lives.

If you're a confused, fearful, or timid parent of children who attend public school, I pray that our journey together will equip and inspire you to get off the bleachers and take an active role in helping your children navigate their public-school years.

GET OFF THE BLEACHERS

As a parent, you're the first-string discipler in your children's faith journeys. From the moment they're born till the day they leave the nest, God has given you the privilege and responsibility to teach them about Him and help them grow their faith in every environment. That's not just my observation. It's a fact, and it's a command from God.

In the Old Testament book of Exodus, the Israelites found themselves entrenched as slaves in Egypt. For four hundred years, generation upon generation lived and died under slavery. Can you imagine? Israelite parents were Egyptian slaves, so their children, then their children's children, then their children's children's children knew no other way of life except the horrors and burden of oppression. Enter Moses, a man God raised up to lead His people to freedom. In answer to their prayers and cries for help, God unleashed a series of plagues and wonders, as only He could do, and delivered His people from Pharaoh's hand. It was an epic rescue that included God parting the Red Sea for His people! When Pharaoh's army pursued them into the sea, the wall of water came crashing down on top of the soldiers and their horses, drowning them all. The account of God's deliverance concludes with these words: "Thus the Lord saved Israel that day from the hand of the Egyptians, and Israel saw the Egyptians dead on the seashore. Israel saw the great power that the Lord used against the Egyptians, so the people feared the Lord, and they believed in the Lord and in his servant Moses" (Exodus 14:30-31).

Undoubtedly, freedom was sweet, but a problem loomed large. Though the Israelites had been set free from slavery, they didn't know how to live as free men and women. So God gave Moses some instructions, including a set of rules known as the Ten Commandments, to guide His people into a right relationship with Him and with one another. The Israelites needed to know how to pass on their faith to the next generation. So the Lord gave them this command: "Hear, O Israel: The LORD our God, the LORD is one. You shall love the LORD your God with all your heart and with all your soul and with all your might. And these words that I command you today shall be on your heart. You shall teach them diligently to your children, and shall talk of them when you sit in your house, and when you walk by the way, and when you lie down, and when you rise" (Deuteronomy 6:4-7).

To further emphasize the importance of God's command to tell their children about Him and help them live out their faith, Moses explained to the Israelites,

> "When your son asks you in time to come, 'What is the meaning of the testimonies and the statutes and the rules that the LORD our God has commanded you?' then you shall say to your son, 'We were Pharaoh's slaves in Egypt. And the LORD brought us out of Egypt with a mighty hand. And the LORD showed signs and wonders, great and grievous, against Egypt and against Pharaoh and all his household, before our eyes. And he brought us out from there, that he might bring us in and give us the land that he swore to give to our fathers. And the LORD commanded us to do all these statutes, to fear the LORD

> our God, for our good always, that he might preserve us alive, as we are this day.'"
>
> DEUTERONOMY 6:20-24

It wasn't a priest's job to pass faith to the next generation; it was the parents' responsibility. This hasn't changed. It's essential that we teach our kids who God is, what He has done for us, and that He is always faithful.

As parents, we're responsible for the daily discipleship of our children. We must connect God to every part of our children's lives twenty-four hours a day, seven days a week. When our children are babies, we help them experience God in what they see, hear, taste, touch, and smell. When they are toddlers, we introduce God to them in every situation, every experience, every challenge. When they are young children, we invite them to trust Jesus throughout their daily challenges. When they are preteens, we help anchor them in Christ so that He might direct every relationship, hope, and dream they have. When they are teens and young adults, we teach and model for them the importance of taking Him everywhere we go—in every situation that requires His wisdom, strength, direction, and provision.

Faith at school starts with faith at home. Honoring this God-given responsibility to our children is essential, regardless of their schooling. While a Christian school may point your children to Jesus, you can't reassign their discipleship. And with the unique challenges kids face in public school, a commitment to the work of discipleship is crucial.

There is no plan B. There is no second-string discipler to nurture your children's faith.

THE "WRONG" ANSWER

One December afternoon, my curly-haired son came barreling through the front door after school, with his coat and backpack flying. My "middle-child blessing," as I call him, was always in motion. Like many other parents, I found snack time around the kitchen table the perfect opportunity to gather information about his day. While he was temporarily sitting still and eating his snack, every day followed a similar routine:

"How was your day?" I'd ask.

"Good," he'd answer quickly, practically dismissing the question.

"Well, what was good about it?" I would say. And that's when the stories came out.

One of my sweet third grader's stories surprised me.

"My teacher said my answer on my paper was wrong," he told me, looking confused. "But it wasn't."

"What was the question?" I asked.

"Write something that describes Christmas," he replied. "I wrote 'Jesus' birthday.' My teacher said that Jesus might be the reason for the season, but we can't talk about Him in school."

What a gut punch. As my son finished his snack, several emotions flew through my mind. First, I was confused. It made no sense to me. Public schools allow children and teachers to talk about Martin Luther King Jr., a famous civil rights leader and a proclaimed Christian, on a national holiday honoring *his* birthday, don't they? Why couldn't a child talk about Jesus in relation to Christmas, the national holiday that honors *His* birthday? Then my momma-bear instinct kicked in, and I became quite angry. With one simple answer, my son's religious freedom was violated. But I was also sad that this kind, loving teacher's response (perhaps unknowingly) hurt my child and her entire class.

I hear many similar stories from parents of teachers who are seemingly misinformed about how to treat expressions of the Christian faith. Their ignorant responses chip away and erode our children's faith and freedom. I wondered, *How could this possibly have happened at my child's public school?*

INACCURATE INFORMATION

As in the case of my son's teacher, one of the biggest threats to our children's religious freedom is the fear spawned from inaccurate information. This lethal combination keeps parents in the bleachers and kids on the sidelines. Whether teachers lack information or dole out the wrong information, the results are the same: Kids' religious liberties in the public-school environment are shut down.

What Are Religious Liberties?

You may not use the term *religious liberties* in your everyday vocabulary, but it's an important concept that appears throughout this book, so I want to take a moment to define it. *In simple terms, religious liberties are specific freedoms that describe your legal right to hold and freely exercise religious beliefs without unwarranted interference by the government.* The First Amendment to the US Constitution further defines and legally protects our religious liberties: "Congress shall make no law respecting an establishment of religion, or prohibiting the free exercise thereof; or abridging the freedom of speech, or of the press; or the right of the people peaceably to assemble, and to petition the Government for a redress of grievances."[3]

These liberties are intended to keep the government neutral, neither helping nor hurting religion but allowing people to practice their religion, or to practice no religion.

My son's teacher had embraced inaccurate information and shut down his freedom to talk not only about his faith but about Jesus as well, likely because she was afraid of getting in trouble. Her words silenced and confused my son. She caused him to believe that it was wrong to describe Christmas as Jesus' birthday.

At the time, I didn't know all I know now about religious freedom. Still, I knew *something* wasn't right. Doesn't the Constitution allow for children to express their personal faith in classwork and homework, provided it fits the context of the assignment?

I had a choice to make. Would I stay quiet or stand up to protect the rights of my son?

I decided to get in the game. I scheduled a time to meet with his teacher and began praying for courage, kindness, and the wisdom to say the right words that would correct this wrong.

When I met the teacher, I approached her with humble curiosity and genuine concern. I thanked her for meeting with me and for her investment in my son and his class. I kindly asked, "Can you please help me understand why you told my son that his description of Christmas as Jesus' birthday was not allowed?"

She was a caring woman and explained that there were children in the classroom who followed a different religion, and she didn't want to offend them. She said she had no idea her response to my son was against any law or policy.

Our Constitution does not recognize the possibility of offending someone as a reason to stifle a child's expression of faith anywhere in the public square, including school. In fact, fear of offense shuts down the freedom of speech and freedom of religion for *all* children in a public school.

This teacher had inaccurate information. Although she was

a terrific teacher and a kind person, she unknowingly presented this misinformation as fact not only to my son and me but to all the families who had children in her classroom as well. After she understood her error, she apologized to both my son and me.

Looking back, I recognize the bravery it took for me to approach that teacher, but it was worth it. My son and I both learned a lesson that day. Getting in the game *works*.

THREE COMMON FEARS

Situations like the one I faced with my son's teacher often create fear and confusion for parents about what to do when our children's religious liberties are violated. We wonder whether it's wrong for our children to mention God in school, or for us to speak up when the teacher is just trying to do his or her job. Questions like these linger in our minds:

- *If I tell my child that his rights were violated, will it steer him down the wrong path?*
- *Will the school and the community label me a "difficult parent" if I say something?*
- *Will my child face repercussions if I intervene?*

These questions reflect three common fears that can keep parents from stepping up to defend their children's religious liberties and discourage kids from expressing a faith that honors God.

1. *The fear of doing something wrong.* Many of us have a healthy fear of breaking the law or violating public-school policies. We want to make sure we know the rules so our

kids can steer clear of getting in trouble with teachers and school staff, which can lead to unpleasant consequences. As Christian parents, we are right in guiding our children to respect authority and seek to follow the rules that teachers establish in their classrooms. But should this fear of breaking rules override the importance of ensuring those rules align with the Constitution? And what if adhering to school rules requires disobeying God and His Word?

2. *The fear of rocking the boat.* Should we intentionally engage in conflict with school administrators? Most parents, including me, don't enjoy conflict, especially with the people we trust with our children's well-being for eight hours a day. We may also be reasonably concerned that pushing back against a school policy might make life more difficult for our kids.

   Whether school administrators and teachers are genuinely mistaken or have a clear anti-Christian agenda, it's never easy to present an opposing view. In the chapters ahead, we'll discuss how best to approach school teachers and administrators. But for now, know that it's worth the effort to seek a fruitful conversation with school staff to nurture your child's faith at school as well as at home.

3. *The fear of not being liked.* The fear of a negative social response—of not being liked—can also hinder us from helping our children live out their faith in public school. We know that friends and neighbors in our school community are watching us, so we may hesitate to take a stand when faced with challenges to our faith. We all want others to like and respect us. So we wonder, *What will others in*

our school community think of me if I take this risk? Will I be categorized as a troublemaker? Will my child be made fun of? Will I be criticized?

WHAT'S AT STAKE?

With these common fears in mind, we must weigh what's at stake for our children when expressions of faith are prohibited at school. In 2003, the Commission on Children at Risk conducted a groundbreaking study on what they called "the crisis of American childhood." It was cosponsored by the YMCA of the USA, the Geisel School of Medicine at Dartmouth (Dartmouth Medical School), and the Institute for American Values. The published report, titled *Hardwired to Connect*, stated that "children's brains are hardwired for a certain level of social and spiritual connectedness. . . . Today's society is lacking in fostering this connectedness, and therefore today's children are suffering. This suffering is linked to an increase in rates of depression, anxiety, attention deficit, conduct disorders, suicidal thoughts, and other serious mental, emotional, and behavioral problems."[4]

The study concluded that children need two kinds of connectedness: "close connections to other people and connections to moral and spiritual meaning."[5] That was quite a revelation in the early 2000s. How much more is it true today? Consider that "16.5% of U.S. youth aged 6–17 experienced a mental health disorder in 2016. This represents more than 1 in 7 youth."[6] Reports of loneliness and suicide rates continue to increase, leading many experts to conclude that youth in the United States are experiencing an unprecedented mental-health crisis. According to Dr. George Barna, director of research at the Cultural Research Center at Arizona Christian University, eighteen- to twenty-four-year-olds today are experiencing severe mental-health problems primarily because they have rejected a biblical worldview and embraced a distorted view of the world.[7]

Based on the results of the *Hardwired to Connect* study, we can conclude that social and spiritual connectedness matter to children. So the benefits of ensuring your children bring their whole selves to school, not needing to compartmentalize their beliefs and values, allow their brains to fire on all cylinders and make deeper connections academically, socially, emotionally, and, yes, *spiritually*. It's imperative that we nurture this need so our kids can flourish at home and at school.

God's Word encourages believers to "walk by faith, not by sight" (2 Corinthians 5:7). The apostle Paul further develops this theme in Romans 12:2: "Do not be conformed to this world, but be transformed by the renewal of your mind, that by testing you may discern what is the will of God, what is good and acceptable and perfect."

Children who feel free to express their faith develop conviction in what they believe and gain the confidence to discuss and defend their faith. Providing them with opportunities to develop their spiritual health and express their faith with continuity wherever they go may be one of the best gifts we, as parents, can give them.

Maybe you're feeling the same way my sidelined football player felt during his first game—intimidated and ill-equipped. Maybe, like my son's teacher, you simply don't know the rules. Perhaps you, like scores of others, feel intimidated by the establishment or the loudest and most confident voices, even though these voices don't necessarily have accurate information. Maybe you, like many parents, long to know the well-defined structure, rules, and guidelines protecting the expression of our children's faith and the best approach for communicating with school administrators when faith and school collide.

Well, don't worry. By the end of our time together, you'll have the tools you need to boldly embrace your role as first-string discipler in your children's faith journeys. It's time to get off the bleachers and help your kids get in the game!

"Leave It!"

A mom was surprised to find a Bible in her son's backpack as he was getting ready for school one morning. Thinking the pack was already heavy enough with the other stuff he needed to take to school, she started to take out the Bible. "No, leave it!" her son responded. "I'm going to read it during my twenty-minute reading time today in class."

CHAPTER 2

UNDERSTANDING THE RULES OF THE GAME

Chase was a freshman in a Midwestern public high school who considered prayer an important part of his day. So important, in fact, that he decided to invite a few friends to pray with him during a free period in the middle of his school day in an empty classroom. Over a period of three years, Chase's student-led prayer group was uplifting and encouraging for those who attended. Students prayed for and with each other during the school day, sang Christian songs, and discussed current events from a Christian perspective. Eventually the prayer group grew to over ninety kids meeting twice a week during free periods. It was so inspirational that even non-Christian students attended.

But was it legal? The assistant principal didn't think so. One day he pulled Chase aside and said that the meetings could continue, but any religious speech would have to stop because of the "separation of church and state." His statement left everyone wondering, *Is this reason valid? Are these students doing something wrong by praying for one another and growing together in their biblical worldview?*

MYTHS, LIES, AND MISCONCEPTIONS

Separation of church and state is one of the most influential and misunderstood phrases in our country. Often lobbed like a grenade meant to stop conversations about faith in public spaces, these weighty words penned by Thomas Jefferson have unfortunately been grossly misused. They have fed the growing myths, lies, and misconceptions that stifle religious freedom in our public square, including our public schools. I could list countless ways public schools protect our kids physically and focus on their intellectual well-being. But when it comes to their faith, the public school's role should be to allow students the freedom to express and live out their faith, not prohibit it. The government is designed to protect religious freedom. This is what makes our nation a beacon of true freedom. Our Founding Fathers fought for it. Our Constitution preserves it. We enjoy it today, and our kids can too. Yet the myths swirling around the "separation of church and state" language can stop our children's religious freedom in its tracks.

Let's talk about three of the most common myths about the separation of church and state and set the record straight.

Myth No. 1: It's in the United States Constitution.

Surprisingly, the phrase *separation of church and state* isn't found *anywhere* in the Constitution, which is the law of our land, including our public schools.

The origin of this phrase is actually a letter Thomas Jefferson, one of our Founding Fathers, wrote on January 1, 1802, to the Danbury Baptist Association of Connecticut. Jefferson penned the following words in response to the association members' confusion over "the legitimate powers of government" with regard to religious expression, the need for well-defined protections of religious liberty, and their opposition to a government-established religion: "I contemplate with sovereign reverence that act of the whole American people which declared that their legislature should 'make no law respecting an establishment of religion, or prohibiting the free exercise thereof,' thus building a *wall of separation between Church & State*."[1]

It's important to note that the phrase *wall of separation between church and state* is *not* included in our established laws. Nor does the Constitution create an impression that the government and religion are exclusive entities that can never touch. They *can* touch, and that is our basis for exercising religious freedom on government property, including public schools. The words *separation between church and state* have been taken out of context and, sadly, misunderstood. Jefferson used this phrase in his letter to clarify and reinforce the fundamental idea that government cannot establish a religion or prohibit citizens from freely exercising their religious beliefs.

Myth No. 2: Separation of church and state means that children cannot talk about God or pray in public school.

The truth is that our children *can* talk about God and pray in public school. Our nation, including our families, is governed by the tenets of the United States Constitution. Embedded in the

First Amendment is the Establishment Clause that addresses our religious freedoms. This important clause ensures our children's right to talk about God, pray, and live out their faith wherever they are. It states that "Congress shall make no law respecting an establishment of religion, or prohibiting the free exercise thereof."[2]

The First Amendment actually shields *the church* from interference by *the state*. It does not prohibit religion from politics, public life, or being an active, vibrant part of each citizen's life or our kids' lives in public school. The government is prohibited from favoring one religion over another or even favoring religion over nonreligion. In fact, our Founding Fathers believed that without shielding the church from interference by the state, there would be no real religious freedom.

Myth No. 3: Separation between church and state means that teachers cannot talk about religion in public school.

The truth is that teachers *can* talk about religion and their own faith, with a few stipulations prohibiting the government, including public-school teachers, from favoring one religion over another or even religion over nonreligion. According to Thomas Jefferson, "The constitutional freedom of religion [is] the most inalienable and sacred of all human rights."[3] Our Founding Fathers further held that belief in God was the key to being good citizens and a great nation.[4] They put religious freedom first for a reason: Its preservation is vital not only to our well-being as a society but also our children's well-being.

Ultimately, the government protects religious freedom by neither promoting nor denouncing any one religion. And public schools, as an extension of the federal government, must do the same. In essence, our kids are free to bring their religion with them into the public square—including public schools! They can practice their faith wherever they are without fear of government censorship or discrimination.

Sadly, the famous words of Thomas Jefferson regarding "a wall of separation between Church & State" have been taken out of context, misunderstood, and misapplied with regard to protecting religious freedom in a public-school setting. School administrators, staff, and families who believe these three myths have become unnecessarily wary of anything religious, for fear they're doing something wrong. Even those with the best intentions misapply Jefferson's words and perpetuate fear that often stifles, paralyzes, and silences our children's freedom of religious expression in school.

When Jefferson's words are correctly applied in light of the Establishment Clause, the meaning becomes clear:

- our schools should not be leading prayer but rather protecting a child's right to pray;
- teachers can teach about different religions, as long as they aren't persuading or compelling their students to believe in one over another; and
- our children's faith doesn't need to be left at the front door of their schools.

Who Was Thomas Jefferson?

Thomas Jefferson has always intrigued me. He was the third president of the United States, one of our nation's Founding Fathers, and the primary author of the Declaration of Independence (at the age of thirty-three). His insight and leadership were vital during a pivotal period in the founding of our nation, and his deep belief in liberty fueled his passion for human rights, including freedom of thought, speech, and religion.

Jefferson took the issue of religion seriously. As a devout deist, he acknowledged a benevolent Creator-God to whom humans owed praise. He was also a big proponent of education and believed it was the path to creating responsible citizens. Jefferson envisioned a robust education system for girls and boys that included primary and secondary schools. Higher education was also a priority of his, and he went on to establish the University of Virginia in 1819. His central role in its planning and architectural design earned him the title "Father of the University of Virginia."

A LESSON FROM DANIEL AND HIS FRIENDS

The book of Daniel, one of my favorite books in the Bible, is not only rich with prophecy—it's rich with examples of how to live your faith in a secular environment. We have so much to learn from the story of one faithful man in a hostile secular environment and how God used him to shape a nation. As we read Daniel's story, God gives us a glimpse into His wisdom as He teaches us how to be courageous in the face of fear, when to speak up and when to be silent, and even how to handle persecution for our faith.

The book begins as Daniel, a Jewish teen from Jerusalem, is ripped from his homeland, along with friends, and carried off as a captive to Babylon. Young Jewish men and women were plunged into a culture of extravagance, wealth, and godlessness. It was quite a culture shock for these teens.

Babylon was an extremely secular culture that didn't honor God, and its king, Nebuchadnezzar, was bent on conquering other nations. Captives were stripped of their identity, and any opposition to the king's reign was met with certain death.

Daniel and his friends Hananiah, Mishael, and Azariah were settling into their new home at the royal palace when Daniel learned that the king had allotted them a daily amount of food and wine from his table. Consuming this food and wine might seem harmless from our contemporary perspective, but it went against sacred Jewish dietary requirements.

So "Daniel resolved that he would not defile himself with the king's food" or wine and asked the chief of the eunuchs to grant Daniel and his friends an exemption (Daniel 1:8).

The man replied, "I fear my lord the king, who assigned your food and your drink; for why should he see that you were in worse condition than the youths who are of your own age? So you would endanger my head with the king" (Daniel 1:10).

After this, Daniel approached the steward who served under the chief of the eunuchs and proposed a test: "Let us be given vegetables to eat and water to drink [for ten days]. Then let our appearance and the appearance of the youths who eat the king's food be observed by you, and deal with your servants according to what you see" (verses 12-13).

The steward agreed to Daniel's proposal, and at the end of ten days, he saw that Daniel and his friends were "better in appearance and fatter in flesh than all the youths who ate the king's food" (verse 15). So the steward let them eat vegetables instead of the king's food.

When Daniel's faith and obedience to God were challenged, he sought to do God's will and confidently lived out his faith in a secular environment. He and his friends surely had the opportunity to speak out about the contradictions between their faith and the Babylonian culture, but they waited on God. Rather than acting in their own wisdom, these teenage boys waited for discernment from God about when to respectfully challenge King Nebuchadnezzar's decree about their faith. The chief of the eunuchs was afraid of a higher earthly authority (the king), but Daniel and his friends had confidence in God's wisdom, power, and ultimate authority. And God blessed their actions.

What encouragement we find in Daniel's story! It seems he was raised in a godly home that equipped him to flourish and grow in wisdom and discernment in a secular environment. You can equip your child to do this too!

WHAT CAN CHILDREN LEGALLY DO TO EXPRESS THEIR FAITH AT SCHOOL?

Your children can legally exercise their religious freedom to a far greater extent than you may realize. When I started researching this topic, I was pleasantly surprised and encouraged that the US Constitution and government guarantee many religious liberties in a public-school environment.

According to the US Department of Education, "Nothing in the First Amendment . . . converts the public schools into religion-free zones, or requires students, teachers, or other school officials to leave their private religious expression behind at the schoolhouse door. The line between government-sponsored and privately initiated religious expression is vital to a proper understanding of what the Religion and Free Speech Clauses of the First Amendment prohibit and protect."[5] This statement is significant. It carries great weight because a government agency has explicitly stated that expressing faith is not restricted in public schools. Guidance from the US Department of Education trickles down to school systems in every state and is a ready defense for parents who feel their children's rights have been violated. It also provides much-needed clarification to parents and school administrators as they work together to ensure that children's religious rights are protected.

This statement reinforces First Amendment protections that guarantee freedom of religious expression. Let's look at three ways our children can freely, and legally, express their faith in public school. (We'll dive into each of these in more detail in the upcoming chapters.)

1. They can express their faith *individually*:

    - Our children have the right to pray when they are not interrupting instruction.
    - Our children have the right to read their Bibles during noninstructional time or when given free choice of reading material.
    - Our children have the right to wear clothing and jewelry with religious messages or icons.
    - Our children have the right to listen to religious music during noninstructional time.

2. They can express their faith *with others*:

    - Our children have the right to organize religious clubs or prayer groups, following the same guidelines as other noncurricular clubs. (*Noncurricular* describes an activity that isn't part of the standard course of study. A Spanish club is curricular; a chess club is noncurricular.)
    - Our children have the right to pray and study the Bible with classmates during noninstructional time.
    - Our children have the right to share their faith with others in a respectful way.
    - Our children have the right to distribute religious literature, following the same school guidelines for distribution of noncurricular literature.
    - Our children may request permission to attend a religious class off campus during school hours.

3. They can express their faith *in the classroom and at school*:

    - Our children have the right to include their faith perspective in classroom discussions and assignments.
    - Our children have the right to engage in respectful debates about religious viewpoints, similar to debating politics.
    - Our children have the right to express their faith at school events, such as talent shows or graduations, provided they maintain control over the content and messaging.

CAN TEACHERS EXERCISE THEIR RELIGIOUS LIBERTIES AT SCHOOL?

One historical fact many parents don't know about is that public schools in America started with religious education. Interestingly, the belief that average citizens should be able to read and understand the Bible for themselves became the catalyst for education in America's original colonies. The Puritans, largely settling in Massachusetts, believed that people must think for themselves about salvation. Those who couldn't read Scripture were dependent on others to tell them what it taught. God was clearly at work during this time, making it possible for laypeople to have access to the Bible.

Exercising their new freedoms, the Puritans set their sights on educating their children using textbooks like *The New-England Primer*, which taught about God and salvation while children learned their ABCs. The Bible, however, was the bedrock teaching tool for all subjects.[6]

The implementation of the US Constitution changed things significantly. As a nation that began with religious freedom, the Founding Fathers wisely underscored and affirmed the premise that personal beliefs can and should be protected. They also realized that the education of citizens was necessary to ensure the success of the nation. So they decided to build on Massachusetts's basic model of education, but without religious instruction. This way, the government could invest in the education of its citizens without being accused of establishing one state-controlled religion.

Today, parents need to be well-informed so we can educate our kids about what forms of religious expression are legal when they walk through the doors of their public school. It's also important to understand the constitutionally protected religious freedoms that our children's teachers have. We need to become "pro-teacher" parents. This means that you assume that teachers have your child's best interests in mind, and you do your best to communicate from that perspective for the well-being of your child. After all, you're on the same team, partnering in your child's educational development and growth.

What is extremely important for teachers and parents to know in this partnership is what public-school teachers can legally do regarding their own freedom of religious expression:

- Teachers have the right to read the Bible and pray when they aren't acting in an official capacity.
- Teachers have the right to teach *about* religion in their classrooms.
- Teachers have the right to accommodate a student's religious rights.
- Teachers have the right to neither encourage nor discourage a student's participation in a religious club or class. (See the appendix for how to find a student's and teacher's "Bill of Rights.")

WHAT CAN I DO IF MY CHILD'S RELIGIOUS RIGHTS ARE BEING STIFLED?

That's a very good question. The religious rights of Chase, the high school freshman at the beginning of this chapter, did appear to be stifled. Chase's story is just one of many examples where students' religious liberties are violated in public schools. But what can you do as a parent to support your child when these situations arise?

The first step is to seek to understand the school policy that is hindering your child's faith expression. Get a printout of the policy and review it carefully to determine the basis for the school's decision. Then determine whether the policy or how the school has interpreted it aligns with the Constitution. Get clarity on this important issue. In many cases, school policies regarding religious expression or how they have been interpreted don't align legally, and further action is needed. (We'll look at some of these cases later in the book.)

The next step is to pray, like Daniel, for discernment and courage to respectfully communicate with school administrators about the misalignment between their policy and your child's religious rights. Stepping up on behalf of your child could be a catalyst that helps the school legally course correct and restores the rights not only of your child but of all the other students as well. Covering the issue in prayer will pave the way for these changes.

Finally, develop a communication plan to kindly educate the educators. In chapter 12, we'll discuss a proven six-step process that will help you do this effectively. The thought of speaking with educators about your concerns can be daunting. But approaching them with kindness, curiosity, and accurate information will start the conversation off on the right foot. Always keep in mind that your intention is to help align the school with the Constitution and ensure your child's religious liberties. Both parties win. It takes intentionality, patience, and effort on your part. But our kids and schools are worth it.

THE REST OF THE STORY

Like Daniel and his friends, Chase and his parents got in the game. They made an intentional effort to address the issue constructively. They researched the high school's policy and determined that the way the school interpreted the policy did not align with the Constitution. Chase's parents wanted their son and his friends to continue their beneficial weekly prayer group during free periods. The policy in question stated that students were permitted to engage in a virtually unlimited variety of activities. And yet the school justified banning religious speech during free periods based on an inaccurate interpretation of school policy as it applied to the "separation between church and state," even though other students were free to spend time together texting on their phones or discussing any other topics.

Chase's parents respectfully explained to administrators that the way the school interpreted their policy clearly violated the First Amendment rights of their son. However, the school district's legal representatives did not agree with the information Chase's parents brought to the table. So Chase and his parents sought advice from Alliance Defending Freedom, a leading legal organization that defends religious freedom and free speech throughout the United States. Their attorneys explained in a letter to the district that the policy violated the First Amendment, which protects the religious speech of students. Unfortunately, Alliance Defending Freedom had to file a lawsuit against the school district in federal court on behalf of this courageous high schooler. Soon after, the court ruled that the school district's censorship of religious discussion and expression during the free period was unconstitutional. Chase's prayer group could continue during their school's free time.

Most of the time, a little discernment and courage, accurate facts, and a respectful conversation with school administrators is all it takes to correct a religious-rights issue. Knowing the rules (school policy), covering the situation in prayer, and kindly educating the educators gave Chase's parents confidence to work toward a resolution. Not only was Chase's religious liberty preserved, but his prayer group was able to continue meeting. Their efforts also ensured that the school couldn't ban any future prayer groups!

In the next few chapters, we'll explore how your children can express their faith individually, with others, and at school. Now that you understand the rules of the game, let's add more tools to your tool kit so you can protect these important expressions of faith.

Magnet Game

At recess, Sean couldn't wait to show his friends the new magnet game he received for Christmas. He dumped a handful of magnets on the table to show how some magnets were attracted to others, and some weren't. He held up a few magnets and proclaimed to his friends, "Let's be like these magnets. Attracted to Jesus!"

PART TWO

Three Ways Children Can Freely Express Their Faith at School

CHAPTER 3

EXPRESSING FAITH INDIVIDUALLY

It was a great first-day-of-school morning at our house. The sun was beaming through the windows as a combination of excitement and jitters danced through the air. My youngest son came to the breakfast table after taking a very long time to get ready. Middle school boys don't usually take much time to get ready, so I knew something was up. I looked at him as he strolled like a proud peacock into the kitchen, and then I knew why he had taken so long. He had meticulously dressed himself from head to toe in yellow-and-green football merch. Everyone who knows him knows he is a die-hard Green Bay Packers fan and has been since he was a young boy. He talks about them to anyone who will listen—and even if they aren't listening. The puzzling thing is that we live in central Pennsylvania, where most people are serious fans of the Pittsburgh Steelers or the Philadelphia Eagles. Our son's displaced passion is a mystery to the family.

My Packers-crazy boy once even sat his father and me down for a serious conversation proposing we move to Wisconsin so he could be closer to the Green Bay Packers. We politely declined his suggestion.

On this first day of school, my youngest son, dressed up in yellow and green, made me smile, but more importantly, he wanted his classmates and everyone around him to know he *believed* in his football team. He *loved* his team. And he wanted everyone to know it before he even opened his mouth. He was quite a sight. His Packers outfit included a green ball cap, cool green sunglasses, an official Packers jersey, yellow shorts, green socks, and flip-flops, all labeled with the official NFL logo of the Green Bay Packers. From head to toe, he was externally expressing his internal faith in his team.

Isn't that the kind of freedom we want our kids—all kids—to have at school when it comes to expressing their Christian faith? Drawing a parallel between our kids' faith in God and faith in an NFL football team is a stretch, I know. But as important as it is for our kids to identify with Christ internally, it's equally important that they have the freedom to express their faith externally as well. Our kids need the freedom to be God fans. As Americans, we've been given the gift of public expression. Kids need to feel safe to identify with Christ in whatever manner they choose.

What our children believe is the most important part of them. Their belief system guides every aspect of their lives. Their choices, their behavior, their friendships, and even their desire to strive for excellence all stem from their beliefs about what is valuable. Faith is an integral part of them, and it will show in their outward behavior. More than a T-shirt or a cross around their necks, their belief in our amazing God and their relationship with

Him should be demonstrated in their speech, their behavior, their dress, and their countenance. I've seen firsthand that when kids realize what Christ has done for them and accept Him as their Savior, in their souls they become raving God fans. Just like my son's Packers fandom, faith in Jesus naturally bubbles out of them. They just can't help it.

We pray our children, like Paul in the New Testament, will declare with their whole hearts, "I am not ashamed of the gospel, for it is the power of God for salvation to everyone who believes" (Romans 1:16).

As their faith spills over into every area of their lives, they will likely want to talk about God and express their growing faith at school. That's part of having a growing faith. But before they can gain the confidence to do so, they first need to understand their constitutional religious rights in a public-school setting.

According to Alliance Defending Freedom, "Students retain their First Amendment liberties while on a school campus. They have the right to share their beliefs, pray, evangelize, read Scripture, and invite students to participate in such activities so long as they are voluntary, student initiated, and not disruptive or coercive. A school may not prohibit student expression during non-instructional time unless it (1) materially and substantially interferes with the operation of the school, or (2) infringes on the rights of other students. A school may not prohibit student expression solely because others might find it offensive."[1]

Buckle up for the ride, because we're going to explore three ways your children can express their faith in public school: individually (privately), with friends, and at school (in the classroom and at school events). First, we'll focus on how they can express their faith individually.

FREEDOM TO BE A GOD FAN

According to the First Amendment, our children are free to be God fans at public school. They can pray silently or aloud, as long as they aren't interrupting instruction. They can choose to read the Bible and other religious materials during their free time. They can wear religious clothing and jewelry to express their personal style. They can even enjoy listening to religious music when appropriate.

Why are these individual expressions of faith so important? As I shared in the previous chapter, children who feel free to express their faith without repercussions develop conviction, the ability to discuss and defend their beliefs (apologetics), and confidence in what they believe. In other words, they're free to be themselves because their faith is an integral part of their lives. But there's another reason. When kids are free to express their faith individually, they are shaping, deepening, and reinforcing a biblical perspective or worldview that will keep them anchored for the rest of their lives.

WHAT IS A BIBLICAL WORLDVIEW?

We all have a worldview, a lens through which we see the world and process our experiences. Our worldview begins to develop after birth, and it's pretty well established by the time we reach our early teens. It shapes our values, our morals, and our character. That's why God commanded parents in the book of Deuteronomy to impress His laws upon their children's hearts. He wants parents to shape their children's worldview based on biblical principles. As Christian parents, we help cultivate a biblical worldview in our children's lives by sharing not only who God is but what He has done in the past, what He is doing in the present, and what He promises to do in the future.

A biblical worldview allows our children to see the world and their experiences at school through God's holy lens, the Bible. This God-focused lens impacts every facet of life, enabling our children to

- value life from the moment of conception,
- understand that God created human beings as either male or female,
- define *marriage* as an exclusive relationship between a man and a woman,
- possess a strong work ethic,
- respect and love others even if they're different from them, and
- demonstrate integrity, doing the right thing even when no one is watching.

These biblical principles often run counter to the messages kids receive from our culture, such as "You are the result of random chance," "You can create your own truth," and "You have no eternal value." The more our children study the Bible and come to know God and His commands, the clearer and sharper their worldview lens will be as they seek to process the world through His eyes. And the better our children process life according to God's wisdom, the healthier they will be.

Let's dive into how our children can express their faith individually in public school. This is not an exhaustive list of their religious freedoms, but it's a great place to start.

The Freedom to Pray

God is great, God is good.
Let us thank Him for our food.
By His hands we all are fed,
Give us, Lord, our daily bread. Amen.

CHILDREN'S PRAYER

Many Christian kids enter their public school with the habit of prayer already deeply ingrained in them. Parents often develop prayer habits early in their children's lives upon which a growing faith is built. Thanking God for their food and praying before bed are usually the first expressions of faith children learn. In fact, prayer is a common faith practice we must teach our children from their toddler years to their teenage years. Prayer is simply talking to God. It can be done anytime, anywhere, silently or aloud. Nineteenth-century preacher and theologian Charles Spurgeon viewed prayer as an "intertwining of his life with that of his heavenly Father in humility and in the certainty of his relationship with Him through the Son. Prayer was not only 'power' and 'sweet converse' with God, but it was also the means whereby daily needs [were] brought to the Throne of Grace."[2]

So what can kids do at lunchtime or any other time during the school day if they would like to talk to God silently or aloud?

From a constitutional standpoint, prayer is considered protected private speech, so children may engage in it at public school as long as the school is not endorsing it. Children can pray privately, such as before meals, as well as with friends. Their freedom to pray comes with two conditions: (1) they cannot pray aloud during instructional time and (2) they cannot disrupt instruction or other activities.

Whether your child desires to pray privately or with a group of friends, student-initiated prayer is legal in our public schools and is a right you can explore further with your child.

First Liberty Institute, "the largest legal organization in the nation dedicated *exclusively* to defending religious liberty for all Americans,"[3] recently shared this report about a public school in Texas:

> Hannah [Allen] and a group of her classmates decided to pray during lunch for one of their former classmates who had recently been in an accident. After initially telling the students, "Y'all don't do that again," Principal Lee Frost told Hannah and her friends they could only pray on the stage behind the curtain, outside of the school building, or in the gym while no one was present. In other words, the students were told that they could not pray in view of the other students. Attorneys from First Liberty informed the school district of the Constitutional rights of Hannah and her friends and requested a clarification of the school's policy. Soon after, school officials corrected their policy. Students, including Hannah, are now allowed to pray publicly.[4]

The Freedom to Read the Bible and Other Religious Materials

Reading time is a favorite among many public-school children. How wonderful it is that children in the United States have the freedom and right to read their Bibles, devotional books, or other religious materials during their free time at school. Don't get me wrong. English and history books are excellent choices that feed the mind, but the Word of God feeds the soul and impacts every part of our children's lives.

Our Founding Fathers allowed for that freedom. As Dr. Benjamin

Rush, a passionate patriot and signer of the Declaration of Independence, affirmed, "The Bible contains more knowledge necessary to man in his present state, than any other book in the world."[5] Even Woodrow Wilson, the twenty-eighth president of the United States, affirmed the crucial value of reading the Bible: "When you have read the Bible you will know that it is the Word of God, because you will have found it the key to your own heart, your own happiness, and your own duty."[6]

What we allow to enter our minds really matters, especially to God. Philippians 4:8 says, "Whatever is true, whatever is honorable, whatever is just, whatever is pure, whatever is lovely, whatever is commendable, if there is any excellence, if there is anything worthy of praise, think about these things." There is a great reward ahead for kids who study and know God's Word.

Kids also have the freedom to discuss with others what they're reading in the Bible. A little boy once told me, "I just can't stop reading the Bible" during his free time at school. He was very interested in what God had to say. He was also excited when his teacher asked him questions about what he was reading, and he shared his thoughts, just as he would when any other book was discussed.

Another elementary-aged boy and a group of his friends decided to read their Bibles at recess and discuss what they learned. Unfortunately, the school principal stopped the student-led Bible discussion. Again, parents and lawyers had to step in and kindly educate the principal to let him know this activity was perfectly legal, and the First Amendment afforded students this right.

The Freedom to Wear Religious Clothing and Jewelry

Kids are kids, and fitting in is paramount to them, especially when it comes to fashion. I remember when my boys were growing up.

It was exhausting trying to keep up with the latest "cool" sneakers. I can't even imagine what it would be like with girls!

When it comes to clothing and jewelry bearing a religious message, Alliance Defending Freedom shares that this type of faith expression is treated as speech, and it can be restricted only in the following circumstances:

- It "materially and substantially interferes with the operation of the school."
- It "infringes on the rights of other students."
- It does not align with school policy.[7]

One article of clothing that has been a fashion statement for American boys and girls since the 1950s—and will likely continue being trendy for many years to come—is the graphic T-shirt. I think it's safe to say that everyone reading this book owns at least one. Graphic T-shirts are comfortable and inexpensive, and they're probably the simplest form of self-expression kids can wear.

A graphic T-shirt gives kids an opportunity to be walking advertisements for the things that are important to them. Kids may wear them just to elicit a laugh or to be noticed, or to show off a product they like or what they believe in. I recently saw a guy at my church wearing a T-shirt that said "SHIRT" on the front, which immediately showed me his brand of sarcastic humor. Our kids have the right to express their faith through a graphic T-shirt.

Jewelry is also a powerful form of self-expression, allowing kids to outwardly communicate their beliefs and personalities without even saying a word. For example, the cross has universal meaning, and many Christians wear cross jewelry as a way of displaying their belief in God and His Son, Jesus.

Just as kids wear clothing and jewelry that express their personalities, especially at school among their peers, they also have the right to wear attire that represents their faith. This freedom of self-expression is protected under the First Amendment.

School officials can't pick and choose which messages students are allowed to express with their attire and which they aren't. That would be considered censorship. If a school allows one type of necklace, all types of necklaces must be allowed, unless a necklace violates the dress code.

It's a general principle that a school that allows any sort of expression in any form during school hours must allow religious expression as well. Students can wear shirts, pants, necklaces, bracelets, and other articles of clothing that display a religious symbol or message, as long as they comply with the school's dress code.

So whether a T-shirt says, "Just Do It," "Jesus Saves," or even "SHIRT," your child can be confident knowing that it's considered freedom of expression, and public schools must allow it when it aligns with the school dress code.

Does Religious Freedom Include All Religions?

Yes! In fact, everyone benefits from religious freedom. The First Amendment protects all people equally—Christians, Jews, Muslims, agnostics, atheists, and others—and preserves the diversity that makes America great. People have different faiths and beliefs, and because we enjoy religious freedom, we can live together peacefully. So when it comes to religion in public schools, a Christian student can wear a cross necklace or study the Bible, a Jewish student can wear a yarmulke or study the Torah, and a Muslim student can wear a hijab and study the Quran without fear of being punished.

The Freedom to Listen to Religious Music

Just like the clothes and jewelry we wear, music is an outward expression of our values and personal preferences. It connects us in profound ways to our shared culture, memories, and experiences. Often, music is an outlet for our emotional health and well-being, reflecting our current emotional state or lifting our spirits.

If we find such deep significance and connection in music, it's easy to understand that a child's freedom to choose the music they listen to during the school day would have an enormous impact on their well-being.

When school administrators offer students a choice of music, our children have the right to listen to Christian songs through their headphones. If other styles of music are permitted during free time or school activities, including school concerts, talent shows, and club gatherings, religious music must be allowed as well. Freedom of choice in music allows our children's brains to fire on all cylinders and make deeper connections academically, socially, and emotionally. In South Carolina, public-school students were asked to pick their favorite songs to perform at a winter concert. Among their choices were "Joy to the World" and "O Come, All Ye Faithful." Unfortunately, the principal banned these songs. Why? The reason given was that if students wanted to play traditional Christmas carols at the concert, they would also have to play songs from other religions. Alliance Defending Freedom attorneys were asked to help. They wrote a letter explaining to the school that "every federal court [asked] to examine the issue has determined that including religious Christmas carols in school music programs fully complies with the First Amendment."[8]

WHAT IF OTHERS ARE OFFENDED?

Some might ask if First Amendment liberties still apply if religious music lyrics are considered offensive to others. What about a religious T-shirt slogan or necklace, for that matter? If a school doesn't want students to wear T-shirts or these other items, they can ban them all. But banning only religious music, clothes, or jewelry crosses the line into unlawful censorship.

Consider the landmark *Tinker v. Des Moines* Supreme Court case in 1969:

> At a public school in Des Moines, Iowa, students planned to wear black armbands at school as a silent protest against the Vietnam War.
>
> When the principal became aware of the plan, he warned the students that they would be suspended if they wore the armbands to school because the protest might cause a disruption in the learning environment. Despite the warning, some students wore the armbands and were suspended.
>
> During their suspension, the students' parents sued the school for violating their children's right to free speech. The U.S. District Court for the Southern District of Iowa sided with the school's position, ruling that wearing the armbands could disrupt learning. . . .
>
> In a 7–2 decision, the Supreme Court's majority ruled that neither students nor teachers "shed their constitutional rights to freedom of speech or expression at the schoolhouse gate." The Court took the position that school officials could not prohibit [the silent protest]

> only on the suspicion that the speech might disrupt the learning environment.[9]

The Supreme Court had ruled for the students and said it didn't matter if people were offended by the black armbands or were suspicious that it might disrupt the learning environment. However, if the students had stood up in the middle of class and chanted, "Stop the Vietnam War," they would have disrupted the operation of the classroom. There is no valid basis for banning religious expression just because someone is offended by or disagrees with a faith message our children express through their clothing, jewelry, or music choices.

So encourage your child to wear that beautiful cross necklace at school or don a favorite Bible-verse T-shirt while listening to uplifting praise music during an appropriate time. The Constitution and the US Supreme Court firmly protect your child's freedom to be a God fan inside and out!

"Repeat After Me"

A third-grade girl was talking at the school lunch table with her friends. One friend shared that she didn't know how to pray, not even the Lord's Prayer. With big eyes, the girl exclaimed, "You don't know the Lord's Prayer?" Her friend shrugged sheepishly. Not missing a beat, the girl instructed, "Then just repeat after me, 'Our Father, who art in heaven . . .'" The friend followed her lead and learned how to pray that day.

CHAPTER 4

EXPRESSING FAITH WITH OTHERS

Dean came from a good Christian family and accepted Christ as his Savior as a young boy. At church, he had many faith-filled friends, and he enjoyed seeing them on the weekend. But the problem was, these friends didn't attend his public school. And the friends he made at his school were a lot of fun, but they didn't share his faith. So Dean had two different sets of friends: one set at church and one set at school. Because a plethora of sports and extracurricular activities filled his weekend schedule when he reached high school, he saw less and less of his church friends. Soon, the only friends he spent time with were those from school who didn't share his faith. He found himself drifting away from God.

"Unfortunately, I drifted so far from my faith that one day, to prove to my thrill-seeking friend group that I was cool and belonged, I foolishly shoplifted small items from a local convenience store," Dean confessed. "I got caught and was taken to the police station. It was awful. The sad part was that I had enough money to buy the items in my pocket." In hindsight, he could see the tremendous negative impact his group of friends had on his thoughts and actions, and ultimately, his faith.

It wasn't until after college that Dean found a friend who was different. This friend was a believer, and he quietly and confidently lived his faith. "He was cool *and* a strong Christian, and he had peace," Dean shared. "I wanted what he had." This friend's influence helped Dean get back on track with his faith and put God back at the center of his life. "I wish I'd been able to find a Christian friend like that in my public school. Things might have been different."

THE VALUE OF CHRISTIAN FRIENDS

Like my friend Dean, many children attending public school have trouble finding friends who share their faith and help them stay on the right track. Some kids feel alone and wonder, *Am I the only Christian in my class? Am I the only one who believes this way?* Maybe your kids have wondered that too.

God has designed His people for community, with Christ at the center. Christian friends not only enhance our faith journeys—they're instrumental in the growth of our faith as well. Christian friendships provide many benefits. The Bible abounds with proclamations of the value of godly friends. Here are just a few of the benefits Christian friends can bring into our lives and the lives of our kids:

- *They help us focus on Jesus.* The account in Mark 2 of the paralyzed man whose friends carefully lowered him on a mat through a roof so Jesus could heal him is incredibly powerful.

Their faith was astounding. Without his friends, the paralyzed man couldn't reach out to Jesus for healing. Christian friends not only keep our kids focused on Jesus; they can bring our kids straight to Him in times of need. Friends remind us that God can and will provide for us, especially in the middle of a tough school day.

- *They encourage and build us up.* First Thessalonians 5:11 says that we should "encourage one another and build one another up." In difficult times when our kids don't naturally turn to us, their Christian friends can encourage and build them up. They need good friends who will pray for them, inspire them to do good works, and are living examples of seeking to please God. Hebrews 10:24 says, "Let us consider how we may spur one another on toward love and good deeds" (NIV).
- *They're honest with us and hold us accountable.* We all need friends who speak the truth to us in love when we veer off course, which for me is often. We need accountability in our Christian walk. We all have blind spots that need correction. Our kids are no different. The apostle Paul warns, "Do not be misled: 'Bad company corrupts good character'" (1 Corinthians 15:33, NIV). But when a Christian friend speaks the hard truth, it edifies us and refines our character. As Proverbs 27 says, "Better is open rebuke than hidden love. Wounds from a friend can be trusted. . . . The pleasantness of a friend springs from their heartfelt advice" (verses 5-6, 9, NIV). As much as we don't like difficult conversations, we all grow from them.

- *Their companionship gives us courage.* According to a 2023 worldview inventory of adults across the United States, only 4 percent held a biblical worldview.[1] That means our kids are in the minority as well! It takes courage for our children to live out their faith in an academic environment where their views are different. Besides being different, even sharing their faith can be scary. Having a Christian friend by their side is priceless during these times. Ecclesiastes 4:9-10 says, "Two are better than one, because they have a good return for their labor: If either of them falls down, one can help the other up" (NIV). I love what Billy Graham said about what it looks like to have strong believers around you: "Courage is contagious. When a brave man takes a stand, the spines of others are often stiffened."[2]

Christian friendships enrich our children's walk with Jesus. Yet sometimes it's hard to find Christian friends at school, and loneliness can set in. So how can godly friends help keep loneliness at bay?

LONELINESS

Loneliness is a growing problem among today's kids. Studies show that feelings of loneliness and isolation are plaguing them. According to *Psychology Today*, "seventy-three percent of Gen Z report feeling alone either sometimes or always."[3] And two-thirds of eleven- to seventeen-year-olds report experiencing stress related to loneliness.[4] Author Jean Twenge states that "U.S. teens' feelings of loneliness began to rise around 2012, just as smartphones became popular and teens started spending less time with each other face-to-face."[5] At the same time, other indicators of teen mental health also began to suffer, with both depression and suicide rates rising. Experts believe that having instant access to technology and social media can prevent kids from making real, personal connections. This is why it's vital that we help our children find Christian friends they can connect with in person at school.

Christian friends can help each other process life through God's lens and cultivate a deeper relationship with Him minute by minute, class period by class period, school year by school year. They can also remind one another that God is always with them—an important truth in combating loneliness.

Scripture tells us, "Whoever walks with the wise becomes wise" (Proverbs 13:20) and "As iron sharpens iron, so one person sharpens another" (Proverbs 27:17, NIV). On life's journey, our kids may feel lonely at times, but Christian friends can draw them back into community. We're all much stronger with Christian friends walking beside us.

What If Your Kids Can't Find Christian Friends?

Sometimes it's difficult for public-school students to find friends who share their Christian faith. Let's face it, we can't control the number of believers attending our children's schools. We can't even control whether any believers at their school will click with them. Sometimes God calls our kids to walk alone for a while, and there is nothing we or they can do about it.

During this difficult time, it's important that we, as parents, help our kids stay close to God and keep a watchful eye as they pray for a Christian friend. It's also important to remind them that God does answer prayer, but sometimes He says, "Wait."

Here are some intentional ways you can help your child during this waiting time:

- Encourage your child to stay involved in a church youth group or Christian activity.
- Spend time with your child and focus on deepening your relationship.
- Invite your child to spend time with Christian friends of yours who are safe adults.
- Pray with your child specifically for a Christian friend and for faith to trust God in the waiting.

HOW CAN MY CHILD AVOID THE DRIFT?

"If you aren't going forward, you're going backward. You can never truly stay in one spot." That is what my dad always used to tell me about life and faith. He said that we tend to drift backward when we don't have a plan to go forward. An intentional plan to develop Christian friends impacts our children's faith foundation so they don't drift. Friends who constantly point us toward the truth of the gospel are priceless.

Have you ever waded into the ocean and tried to stay in one spot? With the strong waves and relentless current nudging you, you don't even realize you're drifting farther down the shoreline away from your favorite beach chair and towel. Within minutes, nothing on the shore looks familiar, and you realize you aren't where you want to be. It's the same with our kids and their faith. Strong waves and gentle currents relentlessly nudge them away from God when they're at school. So as parents we need to do everything we can to help them stay anchored in their faith.

My middle son once told me he didn't think it mattered if

he had Christian friends. So I challenged him to participate in an experiment with me. I asked my son, who is taller and more powerful than I am, to sit on a kitchen chair, while I sat on the floor beside his chair. He represented a faith-filled believer, and I represented a friend who didn't share his faith. I then asked him to shake my hand and try to pull me up to his chair. At the same time, I would try to pull him down to the floor with me.

He chuckled and confidently said, "This is going to be easy!"

"One, two, three, go," I yelled, and then I quickly pulled my son onto the floor.

He was stunned that it was so easy for me to pull him down to where I was sitting. But because of gravity, my pull was naturally stronger. In a tangible way, my son saw that spending time with friends who didn't share his faith could pull him down and weaken his faith over time.

Tough character questions, relationship issues, class assignments pushing popular worldviews, and moral dilemmas all need mental, spiritual, and verbal processing through the lens of God's worldview and the filter of God's Word. Doing this within the confines of safe, trustworthy, gospel-centered friendships makes it harder for our kids to drift.

We see in the Bible that Satan likes to prey on believers who are alone and think they can handle life on their own. It started with Eve in the garden of Eden, where God's words were repeated slightly out of context (Genesis 3:1-6). Instead of asking Adam if what she was hearing was actually what God said, she allowed Satan to fool her by twisting God's words.

Throughout the history of Israel, many kings led the people astray by failing to surround themselves with godly counselors who honored and obeyed God's Word. And in the New Testament, Paul repeatedly instructed the church to guard against false teachers by meeting together faithfully to hear God's Word. God didn't intend for us to walk our faith journeys alone, and that applies to our children as well.

Finding Christian friends and leveraging their positive influence is crucial during our kids' formative years so they'll remain strong in their relationships with God and avoid drifting. Helping our children grow in their walk with God includes making sure they feel free to be themselves and express their faith wherever they are, especially with others.

HOW CAN KIDS EXPRESS THEIR FAITH WITH OTHERS?

Thankfully, the First Amendment legally allows our kids to express their faith with others in public-school settings. This freedom allows them to be themselves with their peers. The added bonus is that when they exercise their religious liberties in group situations, they can find Christian friends who might otherwise remain elusive. Your kids may need your encouragement to participate in or organize group activities centered around their faith. So give them a gentle nudge if they seem apprehensive about expressing their faith with others.

The First Amendment guarantees public-school students the right to express their faith with others in the following ways:

- *Forming religious clubs.* Students can form religious clubs just as they could form any other noncurricular club (like a chess club). Participation in the club must be voluntary, and school rules for student-led clubs must be followed. Like other noncurricular clubs, religious clubs may meet on the school campus during noninstructional time, such as before or after school, during lunch, or during an activity hour.

- *Holding faith-based events at school.* Students can organize prayer groups and gatherings during noninstructional time. These events must be initiated and led by students. One example is See You at the Pole, an annual prayer rally where students gather around school flagpoles before the school day begins to pray for their friends and families, their teachers and their schools, and the nation. This rally is organized and led by students.

- *Praying and studying the Bible with classmates during free time.* Students may pray and study the Bible with fellow students during the school day, abiding by the same terms and conditions that apply to other comparable conversations or activities during free time. They can also participate in events like Bring Your Bible to School Day. Focus on the Family sponsors Bring Your Bible to School Day every October as a way to encourage students to read God's Word and share why their faith is so important to them.

- *Participating in off-campus religious instruction.* Students may be excused from school to participate in off-campus religious instruction taught by nonschool personnel. (I'll share more about this in chapter 9.)

- *Sharing their faith with students of differing religious backgrounds and viewpoints.* Students may share their faith and discuss religious matters with peers in a respectful way, just as they have the freedom to discuss or debate political views.

- *Inviting school friends to church or religious events.* Just as students can invite their friends to a birthday party or a nonreligious event, they're allowed to invite friends to church or religious events. However, they must follow school policies that apply to all events.
- *Distributing religious materials.* Students have the right to distribute religious and nonreligious material at school during noninstructional time, following established policies. They may also post signs on walls and bulletin boards and make announcements about religious events at school, just as they would do for comparable secular events. Schools may not restrict the distribution of literature based on religious viewpoints.

Bring Your Bible to School

Focus on the Family's Bring Your Bible to School Day is an annual celebration that empowers Christian students to live out their faith at school. There are just two simple steps: Young people bring a Bible to school, and then they share with classmates a little about what God's Word means to them! With over a million students participating every October, Bring Your Bible to School Day reminds students that faith is part of who they are—not something to leave at the door. For resources and more information on how your students can participate, go to FocusOnTheFamily.com/Live-It/Bring-Your-Bible.

UNCONSTITUTIONAL SCHOOL POLICIES

Sometimes, public-school policies regarding religious liberties, or how administrators interpret those policies, conflict with the US Constitution. School administrators may violate a student's First

Amendment rights by rejecting a request to freely express their faith at school. Administrators can become even more apprehensive about granting permission for religious expression if a request involves a group of students. That's what happened in one rural Pennsylvania school district.

Student leaders of the Christians in Action Club had a creative idea. They wanted to connect with other students at lunch to discuss thankfulness. The Bible club requested permission to set up a table in the cafeteria for students to sign a poster saying what they were thankful for, and then the club would offer those students a Bible. The table and thankfulness poster were approved, but the principal denied the request to offer Bibles to students.

Unfortunately, even though the Christians in Action Club tried to kindly educate this principal, the parties could not come to an agreement. The principal stood by school policies, which were, in actuality, unconstitutional. The club filed a federal lawsuit against the school district, the superintendent, and the principal for prohibiting students from offering Bibles to fellow students. These policies violated students' speech rights and discriminated against religious speech.

As parents, we need to make sure we know what freedom the law affords our children so we can recognize it and protect it. According to Jeremy Samek, senior counsel for the Independence Law Center, the legal team representing the student leaders of the Christians in Action Club, literature distribution and speech rights should be permitted during the school day at noninstructional times in nondisruptive manners. "Students do not lose their right to free speech when they enter their school," Samek said.[6]

GETTING IT RIGHT: COLSON'S STORY

"Hey, Colson, are you leading worship today?" a friend asked. "Or am I?"

Colson was a young teen who was very involved in his public high school's activities. "I am," said Colson as he swung his black guitar strap over his shoulder to get himself positioned to play.

An hour before the school bell was scheduled to ring to begin the day, Colson and his buddies were ready. They had created a Christian worship service for their peers. Word had spread, and the room was packed with energetic teens excited about worshiping God. The service usually included a time of student-led prayer, a handwritten Scripture verse on a big whiteboard, a short message given by a student speaker or an adult guest speaker, and, of course, worship and praise songs.

The club Colson started at his school is called Fellowship of Christian Students (FCS). This Bible-based Christian club is created by kids for kids, welcoming anyone who wants to attend their independent, student-led worship services. And it's totally legal.

The goals of Fellowship of Christian Students are "to help connect students across the school [who] share the same faith in order to encourage and embolden their faith, to help nurture students' walks in their faith so that they may grow in their understanding and love of God, and to reach out to the students who are curious as to what the Bible teaches so that they may understand what Christians believe."[7]

Recently, when I asked Colson why he likes participating in Fellowship of Christian Students, he grinned at me and said,

"Participating in this group has helped me realize that you can bring faith to every aspect of your life, and I think every moment that you get to share the Word of God, you should take it. Take hold of it and do it because God is everything. Without Him we're nothing."

Colson found friends he might never have met if the First Amendment hadn't afforded him the freedom to form a religious club and host a religious event at school. It took courage and hard work to start a group. And his faith grew as a result. The club also made it easier for Colson to find and connect with faith-filled friends, since worship services attract kids who either have a relationship with God or are seeking Him.

I'm so glad the Founding Fathers allowed for these liberties in the First Amendment so that public-school children can freely express and share their faith with others. Benjamin Rush, who not only signed the Declaration of Independence but was also the founder of Dickinson College, stated, "Freedom can exist only in the society of knowledge. Without learning, men are incapable of knowing their rights."[8]

Remember my friend Dean, who drifted away from the Lord? If Christians at his high school had known about their right to form religious clubs, hold faith-based events at school, or even talk about their faith with others, Dean would have had plenty of opportunities to connect with fellow believers during his school day. And in turn, his faith during his teen years could have flourished instead of deflating.

Let's make sure that opportunities like these don't pass our kids by!

Nothing Is Stopping You

"Bible2School [a public-school ministry] brought the church and school together. And it really opened up the world for me. Church is church. And school is school. *But* they can also be together, and you can spread the Word of God in school. There is nothing stopping you."

COLSON, ALUMNI OF BIBLE2SCHOOL PROGRAM AND A CURRENT HIGH SCHOOL STUDENT

CHAPTER 5

EXPRESSING FAITH IN CLASS AND AT SCHOOL EVENTS

Lydia was nervous as she took the stage with her speech in hand the morning of her high school graduation. She was honored to be asked to give remarks as senior class president and valedictorian. As she looked up from the podium, all eyes were on her. Lydia took a deep, cleansing breath, then launched into her message with confidence. She brilliantly and flawlessly shared what was on her heart with her classmates and their families: her biblical definition of *success*.

Originally, she mistakenly thought success meant being perfect. But getting good grades, making lots of money, and succeeding in a job are all performance-based perfection, not true success as God defines it. Lydia shared what she learned: "My worth isn't found in my successes or my failures. My worth and your worth are found in Jesus, because He is the only One who will ever satisfy us."

Surprisingly, her classmates spontaneously erupted in a roar of applause. Her inspiring speech resonated so much with her schoolmates that it was posted on the internet and went viral, reaching all over the globe. That day, Lydia was bold in her faith. She courageously exercised her freedom to express her faith confidently at a public-school student event.

A lot of parents ask, "Are you sure my child can talk about Jesus in class or at student events?" Although most parents aren't aware of this, the First Amendment does allow students to express their faith and include biblical topics in class assignments, speeches, and student gatherings or events. While this is a protected right, expressions of faith must be student-initiated and relevant to the matter at hand. Before we talk more specifically about these boundaries, let's explore *why* it's important for students to speak up at public school and related events when it comes to their faith.

WHEN KIDS SPEAK UP

At five and six years of age, kids begin school filled with the teaching they received at home. They walk through the school doors with the values caught or taught by those closest to them. If reading has been a priority in their homes, they'll likely value reading. If their families enjoy sports, they often begin school with a deeper understanding of sports than their peers. Likewise, if their families value Christ, prioritize faith, and view a relationship with Jesus as integral to life, they will walk through the school doors with a different worldview from their peers, and it shows.

Like Lydia, all kids bring prior knowledge and convictions with them into speeches, assignments, and learning situations. This integration is part of healthy learning. When children have the opportunity to freely make connections with *all* the information and perspectives they possess—including their faith perspective—their discussion and understanding of the proposed subject matter or idea *increases*, and healthy learning takes place.

Socially, it was risky for Lydia to stand up and share her beliefs with her classmates in such a public way. It required courage to reveal her core beliefs and talk about the truth found in God's Word. It was not only brave but loving. Her peers really will find no satisfaction or worth apart from Jesus. But was Lydia's speech merely evidence of an outgoing personality? Or did she develop her boldness for Christ at home? Should we, as parents, encourage our kids to speak up publicly about their faith? Is it important for them to articulate their faith? Should we encourage them to dig into the Bible for a class assignment or research a person of faith in history for a project? Should we encourage them to share Jesus in a commencement speech?

The answer may be challenging, but it really is simple.

Yes. We must encourage our kids to explore the vastness of God's creation and wisdom in learning and to practice articulating their beliefs and worldview. Learning to share their faith is an important part of discipling our kids. And as we talked about in chapter 1, we have been given the responsibility and privilege of being our children's "first-string" discipler. Learning to see God's hand in the secular and the sacred is our job as parents. And teaching our kids how to share their faith is our responsibility.

In Mark 16:15, the very last words of Jesus on earth to His disciples were "Go into all the world and preach the gospel to all creation" (NIV). Notice that this is a command and not a suggestion. Following Jesus will involve articulating the gospel, or good news about Jesus, to the world. So how will our kids tell others about Him publicly if they never learn to do so or practice this skill? We must teach them how to articulate matters of faith by discussing faith with them. When our children talk about God at home, it grows their faith. When they share their beliefs to their friends, it refines their faith. When they express their faith in public, it matures their faith.

I had the opportunity to disciple my oldest son in learning to express his faith during a persuasive-composition class in high school. The class stretched him in his educational learning as well as his faith. Each week the teacher would assign a controversial topic to the class. Students would then pick one side of the debate to defend in writing and in their class discussion. Abortion, animal rights, environmental issues, and gay rights were all hot topics on which my son wrote his persuasive essays. Each week he chose the side of the debate that aligned with his biblical worldview. The majority of the time he was alone in his stance. And it was difficult. Yet being forced to articulate his faith in both writing and class discussions transformed my son. He owned his faith in God in new and dynamic ways. As I reflect on that trying season, I can clearly see three ways God grew my son:

1. *My son understood and owned his faith.* Before articulating his faith in writing or verbalizing it to others, he first needed to solidly know what he believed and why. This required deeper thought and research. It prompted conversations about difficult topics at home that needed to be fleshed out with the truth of Scripture taught by parents who loved him. He asked hard questions. This deep work ignited a new passion in him about his faith.

2. *My son courageously articulated a countercultural viewpoint with his peers.* As my son seized the opportunity to grow his faith, this class gave him a platform to respectfully share an

alternate point of view than the one our culture promotes. This view was based on the truth of Scripture that his classmates might not otherwise have considered or even heard. It was a relatively safe way to learn not only to articulate an unpopular viewpoint without shrinking back but also to disagree and still respect his peers.

3. *My son explored the ways his faith intersects with all areas of his life.* He learned that God's authority, character, and love intersect with every aspect of life. Embracing a biblical worldview isn't always popular, but Scripture is still relevant and speaks to matters he faces today. His faith deepened by asking and answering questions like *What does God say about that?*, *What does that tell me about God?*, and *How can I convey this in a way that engages others?*

In Acts 4:12, Peter proclaimed publicly, "Salvation is found in no one else, for there is no other name under heaven given to mankind by which we must be saved" (NIV). My son was very thankful he had the freedom to proclaim this truth by sharing his faith in the classroom. Whether your children choose to share their faith boldly or with small baby steps, there is no doubt their walk with Christ will be transformed when they speak up at school.

THE FREEDOM OF RELIGIOUS EXPRESSION

When citizens are allowed to express their thoughts and ideas publicly, true freedom flourishes. According to Grant Atkinson of Alliance Defending Freedom, "Allowing everyone to freely express their beliefs is a hallmark of any free society. . . . In a society governed by free speech, bad ideas can be countered with positive and truthful ones. Robust debate is essential to determining which ideas are true and good, and when more people speak up for the truth, false and worthless statements are recognized for what they are."[1] In essence, our kids can contribute to a healthy learning environment by exercising their religious liberties. Thankfully, the Constitution allows for these liberties as long as the students have an educational purpose in sharing their beliefs and comply with school rules.

Let's explore how the broader freedom of expression that Grant Atkinson was referring to applies to expressing faith in the classroom and at student events.

Kids can legally exercise their freedom of religious expression in three ways:

1. *Sharing their faith and biblical references in class assignments.* Students can talk about their faith in any class assignment as long as the information they're contributing is relevant to the topic at hand and meets the requirements of the assignment. For example, kids can create a book report or an oral essay on Jesus, Moses, or any influential person who reflects their faith. If a class assignment is to take a popular song and turn it into a poem, your child can pick a Christian song. If an art teacher gives an assignment to paint a scene from history, your child could paint any historical scene from the Bible, like the crucifixion. The Bible can also be referenced in a writing assignment. After all, it is the most influential book in history!

2. *Discussing their religious viewpoints.* Similar to debating politics or which football team will win the Super Bowl, our children have protected speech when it comes to discussing their faith. They can share their biblical worldview

one-on-one or in a classroom of peers. They can discuss hot topics like gender identity, evolution, or the value of life. They can respectfully disagree with a teacher over popular views on marriage that oppose what the Bible teaches, engage in a discussion with friends on what Jesus says about salvation, and ask thoughtful questions that invite discussions about faith. Be assured, the First Amendment makes it legal for your children to discuss their religious viewpoints in public school.

The First Amendment

The First Amendment to the United States Constitution protects religious liberty and rights related to freedom of speech. Found in the Bill of Rights, this amendment prohibits the government from adopting laws that would establish a religion (frequently called the Establishment Clause), as well as laws that would forbid the free exercise of religion (also called the Free Exercise Clause). The First Amendment also expressly protects freedoms of speech, the press, peaceable assembly, and petition to the government. We should be grateful for an amendment that affords us so much freedom. The Founding Fathers, in their great wisdom, placed this amendment first in the Bill of Rights because it's the foundation of a truly free society.

3. *Expressing their faith at student events.* Kids are permitted to talk about God when giving speeches at student events, including high school commencement speeches. According to First Liberty Institute,

> Students can include religious content, including prayer, in their graduation speech if: Students are

> selected by neutral criteria[,] . . . [and] control over the content of each address is left to the students—not the school. . . . For example, if the school allows the valedictorian, salutatorian, class president, and class vice president to each speak for a certain amount of time, and the students have control over the content of their speeches, then the school cannot discriminate against students who wish to incorporate religious speech, including prayer, in their addresses.[2]

Unfortunately, school officials sometimes mistakenly suppress these student-initiated expressions of faith in school assignments, discussions, and speeches, which can undermine learning.

HOW SUPPRESSION OF RELIGIOUS FREEDOM HURTS LEARNING

Benjamin Franklin, inventor and signer of the Declaration of Independence, said, "Without freedom of thought, there can be no such thing as wisdom; and no such thing as public liberty, without freedom of speech."[3]

Suppression of religious liberty can happen when educators prohibit students from expressing their faith in their school lives. Situations where this occurs can be overt or subtle. An overt example of suppressing religious liberty is when a teacher allows all the children in the class to bring their favorite book from home to read at Easter, and one child's choice of *The Tale of Peter Rabbit* by Beatrix Potter is welcomed but another child's choice of *The Very First Easter* from *The Beginner's Bible* is prohibited. Or when students are allowed to sing a Taylor Swift song at a school talent show but not a worship song.

An alarming trend in our culture today is that any speech that conveys a different point of view from our own is considered objectionable. As a result, free speech is often suppressed and considered dangerous. Surprisingly, some people in our country are even starting to view the censoring of speech favorably.

According to a study by the Foundation for Individual Rights and Expression and the Polarization Research Lab at Dartmouth College, 53 percent of adults surveyed said the First Amendment "goes too far in the rights it protects."[4] This trend is dangerous. It isn't just unconstitutional; it negatively impacts the development of our children academically, and it sets an alarming trajectory for the future. Limiting the freedom to incorporate faith-filled ideas and thoughts into their academic journeys hurts every child in public school, not just our own children. Kids (and adults) in our society need to learn how to listen and disagree respectfully! Ultimately, suppression of differing ideas squelches freedom of choice, impedes critical thinking, and stifles creativity for all children. Let's take a closer look at each of these.

Squelching Freedom of Choice

When our children aren't allowed to pick something religious for a class assignment, a project, or school activities, their freedom of choice is squelched. Matt Sharp, a lawyer with Alliance Defending Freedom, represented a student named Brian Hickman, whose freedom of choice was violated. Here's the story Matt shared with me:

> You may not think a fifth grader with cerebral palsy who wanted to dance at his school talent show could ignite

a battle over free speech and religious liberty, but that's probably because you haven't heard of Brian Hickman.

At family get-togethers and parties, Brian wanted to be the first one on the floor, dancing and jumping to the music. Brian's mom, Adriana, had taught Brian from a very young age to never let his cerebral palsy keep him down, and he took that advice with him on the dance floor and everywhere else he went.

When his Los Angeles elementary school put on a talent show, Brian knew what to do. For weeks, a church music team had been teaching Brian a dance to a contemporary Christian song called "We Shine." Excited to show what he had learned, Brian performed the dance at his school's auditions.

Brian couldn't wait to show off his moves to a live audience of fellow classmates, their parents, and community members who would come out to the voluntary event—scheduled for two weeks after auditions. Plus, with a major hip surgery scheduled just a couple of weeks after the talent show, this was going to be one of Brian's last chances to dance for the foreseeable future.

Yet, several days later, Adriana got a call. School officials were refusing to let Brian dance to the song he chose. When Adriana spoke with the school principal, she was told the song said "Jesus" too many times.

As they talked further, the principal told Adriana that the song was considered . . . "offensive." Adriana was also told that Brian's dancing to the song would be a violation of the so-called "separation of church and state"—a phrase that is frequently used by school officials to restrict students' private religious speech even though it is found nowhere in the Constitution.

Keep in mind, other students were free to choose their own songs, dances, or other talents to perform at the show. Brian's classmates were planning to dance and sing to everything from classics like "Eye of the Tiger" to popular songs by Selena Gomez and Miley Cyrus. Performances included songs [that involved] teenage romance, relationship problems, dancing, and violent imagery.

The only song deemed inappropriate was the one with too many references to Jesus.

Adriana wasn't looking for confrontation. She pointed out to the principal that the only songs Brian listened to were worship songs, so if he picked another song it would still be faith based, but she still relayed the news to Brian and asked him if he would be willing to choose another song.

Brian was heartbroken. He couldn't grasp why the school wouldn't let him dance to a song that mentioned Jesus. Through tears, he told his mom that since he had already worked so long and so hard on "We Shine," the thought of starting from scratch with another song was too crushing [for him] to move forward.

With the talent show just a week away, Adriana made a deal with her son. If Brian kept working on his song, she would do what she could to give him the chance to perform [it]. Adriana called Alliance Defending Freedom, and together, they filed a lawsuit against the Los Angeles Unified School District.

> Within days, the school reversed course and announced it would allow Brian to perform his song. And it even revised its policies so that other students [will] never face the same restrictions if they choose to use a religious song at a school talent show.

Public schools can't pick and choose which of their students have the right to free expression. And officials can't censor students' speech on public-school campuses. That's at the heart of what the First Amendment protects. Yet First Amendment violations like these are all too common at public schools across the nation.

Thankfully, the Los Angeles Unified School District did the right thing in time for Brian to perform at the talent show—for which he received a standing ovation from the community.

Besides the squelching of our children's freedom of choice through the unnecessary suppression of faith, we must also consider how censorship impacts the learning process.

Impeding Critical Thinking

Most educators agree that fostering and encouraging critical thinking in the classroom is a crucial element in a child's educational experience. Critical thinking occurs when students analyze, evaluate, interpret, and process information and apply creative thought to form an argument, solve a problem, or reach a conclusion. When children bring their viewpoints into classroom discussion, including their thoughts on God, it impacts the student body as a whole. It opens up the world of knowledge and makes it available to *all* students, enhancing everyone's critical-thinking opportunities.

The children's classic *Alice in Wonderland* is a great example of how limiting perspectives impacts critical thinking. In the story, Alice lets curiosity get the best of her and follows an elegantly dressed talking rabbit down a rabbit hole. She later drinks a liquid that shrinks her, because she is too big to fit through a mysterious door. Alice has the opportunity to explore a new perspective when she shrinks. Instead of embracing, enjoying, and engaging with a new perspective, she complains to the caterpillar that she wishes to be more than three inches tall. Her new reality is unfamiliar and uncomfortable. Confused, the caterpillar replies that three inches is a very good height (as he was exactly three inches tall). Alice's plea parallels the reaction we naturally have when we encounter ideas that make us feel uncomfortable.

Real learning and critical thinking are full of uncomfortable moments. When we move to the safety of comfort rather than curiously exploring an idea and gaining a new perspective, no one's thinking is stretched, and learning is one-dimensional. While it is vital to align our perspectives with the Word of God, we won't grow in a vacuum chamber of our own ideas. Likewise, people won't find or learn about faith if no one ever speaks up.

Stifling Creativity

Because art is a student's personal expression, not the school's, it is subject to full protection under the First Amendment. Anthony's story illustrates how creativity can be stifled in public schools:

> Anthony, a senior at a high school in Wisconsin, drew a picture for art class with a road, a cross, and the words "John 3:16—a sign of love." It was his favorite verse, and he was surprised when his art teacher told him to remove it. Anthony refused to alter his artwork. The teacher

decided to give him a zero for the assignment because of the religious content of his drawing and the potential for offending other students. Thankfully with the help of Alliance Defending Freedom, Anthony filed a lawsuit to challenge the censorship of the religious message in his artwork. Shortly thereafter, the school district agreed to settle the case.

Our Founding Fathers knew that aligning expressions of faith at home and at school is healthy for kids because it brings continuity to their world. Samuel Adams, a leader of the American Revolution and signer of the Declaration of Independence, wrote, "The right to freedom being *the gift* of God Almighty . . . *the rights of . . . Christians* . . . may be best understood by reading—and carefully studying—the institutes of the great Lawgiver . . . which are [clearly] written and promulgated in the *New Testament*."[5] Freedom, a gift from God, is understood more clearly through the reading of His Holy Word. Our children's faith is part of who they are and how they think. They don't need to leave it at the front door of their public school.

When a violation of a child's religious rights occurs, often all that is needed to clear things up is a conversation that kindly educates the educators. Sometimes, however, a legal challenge may need to be pursued. Regardless, our children's freedom to express their faith at school, when appropriate, needs to be upheld and taken seriously. Our children shouldn't fear suppression or punishment when they express their faith in class or at student events. Making sure everyone stays in their legal lanes benefits our children and ultimately our schools. As parents, we want to partner with public-school administrators in the education of our children to ensure that all kids have freedom of religious expression and an environment where they can flourish and grow.

Questions on the Bus

Samuel: "I want to go to heaven, and I want to know how to believe in God."
Colson: "This is how you believe in God. First of all, you have to believe in Him and accept Him into your heart."
Samuel: "But how do I do that?"
Colson: "You can pray to God to accept Him into your heart."
Samuel: "Can you pray with me?"
Colson: "Sure!"

PART THREE

Unique Spaces for the Bible in Public School

CHAPTER 6

HOW THE BIBLE CAN TRANSFORM KIDS' LIVES

Kids armed with a love for God and His Word can change a nation.

Josiah was eight years old when he became the king of Judah. Surely he was surrounded by adult advisers, because I've raised three eight-year-old boys, and they couldn't remember to do their homework without help, let alone run a nation. Somewhere in the mess of his father's funeral and his grandfather's devastatingly evil legacy, young Josiah had someone tell him about the one true God.

I wonder if those people whispered to him about the God of his ancestors and the former glory of the nation under King David like telling a fairy-tale bedtime story, or if they spoke openly in an advisory meeting. Regardless, King Josiah embraced the God he knew only secondhand. This devotion led him to begin repairs on the Temple in Jerusalem, which was in shambles. His grandfather Manasseh had reigned fifty-five years, bringing unspeakable evil into the Holy Land. Child sacrifices, mediums, and idols representing false gods were all evil, and everything that was holy unto the Lord had been desecrated. This included the Temple of God.

Josiah was twenty-six years old when he received word that the high priest had found a book in the Temple. But it wasn't just any book; it was the Book of the Law that had been lost for two generations. As the secretary began reading the words aloud to Josiah, the king tore his clothes in fear and grief. Knowing the sin of his people was great, he said to the secretary, "Go, inquire of the Lord for me, and for the people, and for all Judah, concerning the words of *this book* that has been found. For great is the wrath of the Lord that is kindled against us, because our fathers have not obeyed the words of *this book*, to do according to all that is written concerning us" (2 Kings 22:13, emphasis added). God's response was swift: "I will bring disaster upon this place and upon its inhabitants, all the words of *the book* that the king of Judah has read. . . . But to the king of Judah, . . . thus shall you say to him, Thus says the Lord, the God of Israel: . . . Because your heart was penitent, and you humbled yourself before the Lord, when you heard how I spoke against this place and against its inhabitants, . . . I also have heard you" (verses 16, 18-19, emphasis added).

The Word of God is transformative and brings blessing. Josiah now knew how God wanted him and all Israel to live, and it changed everything. Immediately, King Josiah removed all traces of the pagan culture and recommitted himself and all Judah to the Lord: "The king stood by the pillar [of the Temple] and renewed the covenant in the presence of the Lord—to follow the Lord and keep his commands, statutes and decrees with all his heart and all his soul, thus confirming the words of the covenant written in *this book*. Then all the people pledged themselves to the covenant" (2 Kings 23:3, NIV, emphasis added).

The Word of God really can change lives. Because Josiah read and lived the Scriptures, he enjoyed the blessing of God on his life and his nation during his lifetime. God's Word tells us that "neither before nor after Josiah was there a king like him who turned to the LORD as he did—with all his heart and with all his soul and with all his strength, in accordance with all the Law of Moses" (23:25, NIV).

It's a great story made even greater because it's true, but why is it so important today? What kind of impact can engaging with the Bible really have on your child's life? What is Bible literacy, and why is it so important?

BECOMING BIBLE LITERATE

The fundamental barrier to a relationship with God is not knowing the truth about who He is or what He has done for us. God's Holy Word holds those rich truths for anyone who reads and studies it. The kingdom of Judah was lost spiritually because the Holy Scriptures were lost. No one had access to them. They needed to find God's Word, read it, internalize it, and obey it to literally save their nation. Gratefully, the Bible we have today isn't buried under the debris of a temple in disrepair, as the Jewish Bible was in Josiah's day. It's readily available to our kids. The goal is that they become Bible literate—a precursor to building faith in Christ.

What exactly is Bible literacy? It's simply the ability to read and understand the Bible. It begins with reading, absorbing, and being able to recall the major narrative of the Bible, which encompasses the Old and New Testaments. Literacy doesn't require our kids to agree with what they read—faith is, after all, born in the heart. But it does allow them to read the Bible with enough understanding to explain its basic meaning. Truly biblically literate people, like those who study other literature, learn how to read with a heart to understand, appreciate, and create meaning about life, God, and the world. Don't miss this; it's incredibly significant! When our kids read and study the Bible, they don't just gain knowledge; they are introduced to their Creator and His plan for them.

Scripture is clear about why all this is important: "Faith comes from hearing, and hearing through the word of Christ" (Romans 10:17). With Bible literacy in their wheelhouse, our children can find the pathway to faith. Our role as parents is to read, speak about, and teach God's Word to our children every chance we get. We're also called as first-string disciplers to provide them with a factual, godly framework for processing life's issues. Though we can't instill faith in our children, we can equip them to know the God of the Bible. As our kids hear God's Word regularly, seeds of faith are planted and begin to germinate in the fertile soil of God's Word. Bible literacy is the trellis that enables our children's faith to grow upward and outward.

Teaching our children the Scriptures not only removes barriers to a relationship with God, but it also transforms lives, like Josiah's. Let's look at three ways transformation happens: spiritually, behaviorally, and educationally.

Spiritual Transformation

Our kids' salvation and eternal destination are what keep us up at night as parents. Spiritual transformation is the key to unlocking the gift of eternal life that God promises in His Holy Word. Reading the Bible is often the first step in this journey. Abandoning the Scriptures and its truths inevitably leads to evil and ruin for a nation and its people, as Josiah realized with deep grief. In Romans 8:5, the apostle Paul wrote, "Those who live according to the flesh set their minds on the things of the flesh, but those who live according to the Spirit set their minds on the things of the Spirit." This resetting of the mind that Paul is talking about is the transformation we long for our kids to experience.

Let's talk adult to adult for a moment. What is this message of salvation or becoming "saved" that we all need to hear, absorb, and live? Dr. George Bethune, a nineteenth-century theologian, gives us a simple way to understand the salvation message Paul explained in the book of Romans. According to Dr. Bethune, salvation involves three words: *guilt*, *grace*, and *gratitude*.[1]

Guilt is the realization and humble admittance that "all have sinned and fall short of the glory of God" (Romans 3:23). I remember the first time I heard these words and became not only aware of being a sinner but also that I wasn't alone. We *all* fall short of perfection. Only God is perfect, and so we, as sinners, can't be with Him in heaven for eternity. This is the destination problem we all have. We also have a problem here on earth, because our sin has separated us from God and from one another (Isaiah 59:2; Romans 3:10-12). So I can wake up in the morning to enjoy a peaceful tea and toast before my kids awaken. But by the time the morning routine has started, I've yelled at two children fighting, slammed a door, and snapped at my husband before I've even finished packing all the lunches. Yes, as humans we are perpetually sinful. We deserve the punishment of death (Romans 6:23), which is eternal separation from God. But then *grace* enters.

Grace is what God showed us in sending His Son, Jesus, to earth. Grace is getting something we don't deserve, when what we actually deserve is death. On the cross, Jesus took the death sentence for our sin to reconcile us to His Father! His grace covers all our sins, even the plethora of sins I committed all before eight o'clock in the morning. In Romans 5:7, Paul said, "Very rarely will anyone die for a righteous person, though for a good person someone might possibly dare to die" (NIV). Yet Jesus paid the price for my sin and yours with His life, taking away the death sentence we deserved. My heart is full when I think that Jesus loved us so much that He willingly died in our place, "the righteous for the unrighteous" (1 Peter 3:18). Then He rose from the dead, assuring us of eternal life in heaven when we come to Him in faith for our salvation.

In a world filled with lies, the Holy Spirit reveals in the Bible the truth that we can't make ourselves perfect. I can't save myself from my own sins no matter how hard I try. But in His amazing grace, God had the perfect plan to save us through His Son. And we don't deserve it. That's where *gratitude* comes in.

Gratitude culminates in living a life according to God's will. With the help of the Holy Spirit, we are grateful for God's gift of eternal life through grace, and we live accordingly. As we learn more about who God is and how He calls us to live by studying His Word, the more we desire to live a life pleasing to God. The goal, as Colossians 1:10 states, is to "live a life worthy of the Lord and please him in every way: bearing fruit in every good work, growing in the knowledge of God" (NIV).

This message of salvation in the Bible is vital information for our children that can spiritually transform them. We can't let them miss it. It's essential that we remember we are still just one generation from the Word of God being lost to our children and grandchildren. As first-string disciplers in the lives of our children and ones who bear the responsibility of sharing the salvation message that brings spiritual transformation, we must help our children access and understand the Word of God. Interestingly, in addition to spiritual transformation, serious behavioral transformation also takes place that even secular research can't deny.

Behavioral Transformation

We love to see our kids growing spiritually as they read, study, and absorb the Bible. But did you know their behavior can actually be *transformed* by reading the Bible? Yes, according to the Center for Bible Engagement, the research shows a profound difference in people's lives when they engage with the Bible four or more times a week:[2]

> *Emotional benefits*: Our kids become emotionally resilient as God fills their hearts with peace through His Spirit (Galatians 5:22). The results:
>
> - Odds of "experiencing loneliness" drop 30 percent.
> - Odds of "lashing out in anger" drop 31 percent.
>
> *Behavioral benefits*: Our kids respect vital safety guardrails as they discover the life-transforming power of "[offering their] bodies as a living sacrifice, holy and pleasing to God" (Romans 12:1, NIV). The results:
>
> - Odds of "drinking to excess" drop 62 percent.
> - Odds of viewing pornography drop 59 percent.

> *Relational benefits*: Our kids follow godly guidance for healthy relationships and seek to live out God's command to "love your neighbor as yourself" (Matthew 22:39, NIV). The results:
>
> - Odds of "having sex outside marriage" drop 59 percent.
> - Odds of "feeling bitter" drop 40 percent.
>
> *Spiritual benefits*: Our kids experience greater spiritual growth and expand in their ability to share their faith. They begin caring more about the spiritual condition of others and Jesus' command to "make disciples of all nations" (Matthew 28:19, NIV). The results:
>
> - Odds of "feeling spiritually stagnant" drop 60 percent.
> - Odds of sharing one's faith with others jump 228 percent.
> - Odds of discipling others jump 231 percent.

Isn't this the kind of positive behavior we want for our children? In a time of overwhelming mental-health issues and loneliness plaguing this generation, what if we could offer them true hope? These research results are encouraging news for families. But there's more.

Educational Transformation

Did you know that engaging with the Bible makes kids smarter? Dr. William Jeynes, senior fellow at the Witherspoon Institute in Princeton, New Jersey, and a professor of education at California State University in Long Beach, conducted a study indicating that students with high Bible literacy perform better academically than those with lower Bible literacy. He concluded,

> It is also likely that Bible literacy has a spiritual and moral influence on young people that [leads] to their doing better in school. To the degree that the Bible encourages people to have a sense of purpose, to be disciplined morally and otherwise, and to feel loved and valued by God, one would expect that when a person reads and applies the Bible, academic improvement will follow.[3]

It's true. When we know God loves us and has a purpose for our lives, we do better in life. Dr. Jeynes's fascinating secular meta-analysis of the research also concluded that Bible literacy can increase kids' overall GPA by 0.6 points on a four-point scale![4] For example, student grades would increase from a 2.4 to a 3.0. That's like going from being a C-plus student to a B student or a B-plus student to an A student just by becoming biblically literate. This is amazing!

The Bible promises wisdom to those who treasure the Word of God. As parents, we long for our children to have lives brimming with the goodness of the Lord in all areas. The Bible itself outlines the benefits of immersing our kids in Scripture:

> The law of the Lord is perfect,
> reviving the soul;
> the testimony of the Lord is sure,
> making wise the simple;
> the precepts of the Lord are right,
> rejoicing the heart;
> the commandment of the Lord is pure,
> enlightening the eyes;

the fear of the Lord is clean,
    enduring forever;
the rules of the Lord are true,
    and righteous altogether.
More to be desired are they than gold,
    even much fine gold;
sweeter also than honey
    and drippings of the honeycomb.
Moreover, by them is your servant warned;
    in keeping them there is great reward.

PSALM 19:7-11

We long for our children to have wisdom, joy, and insight. Just like King Josiah and the psalmist's experience, when our kids engage in the Bible, they enjoy far-reaching life benefits. This is our earnest prayer for them. As the first-string disciplers of our children, we can help set them on that path.

FEAR NOT

So many Christian parents I talk to are fearful because they want to immerse their children in the Word of God, but they think that studying the Bible has no place in their kids' week at public school. They've been wringing their hands for years, feeling hopeless and helpless because they see more and more darkness seeping into our public schools. I can understand why they feel that way. But here are three things we need to keep in mind as we process the issue of faith and the Bible in the public-school environment:

1. People cannot take God out of any place; He is everywhere.

2. We must not let fear drive this conversation; God is in control.
3. We need to take advantage of the opportunities that have been afforded to us legally; God gives us all we need.

Here's a quick recap of what we know about the history of religious rights in public school:

- In 1789, public schools started removing *the Bible* from curriculum to ensure the government could not establish a religion.[5]
- In 1962, the Supreme Court ruled that school-sponsored *prayer* violated the Establishment Clause.[6]
- In 1963, the Supreme Court ruled that school-sponsored *Bible reading* for religious and moral instruction violated the First Amendment.[7]
- In 2000, the Supreme Court ruled that public schools violated the Establishment Clause by "permitting student-led, student-initiated" *prayer at football games*, since it "involved both perceived and actual government endorsement" of prayer at school events.[8]

Given that list, it looks like the Bible was removed. But it wasn't. Kids didn't lose their religious rights. They are still intact. The real lesson in our history is that public-school teachers and administrators were legally taken out of the picture as Bible facilitators and prayer leaders in our children's lives. Yet discipleship was never their job to begin with; it is our job as parents and first-string disciplers!

The government has never truly taken the Bible or prayer out of our children's hands. As you look at the religious practices that historically have been removed from public school—school-sponsored curriculum infused with the Bible, school-sponsored prayer, and school-sponsored Bible reading—let's remember these four things are *still* true for our children in public schools:

1. Kids *can* express their faith in their school curriculum.
2. Kids *can* pray in school.
3. Kids *can* read the Bible in school.
4. Kids *can* pray or read the Bible at student events.

Opportunities to live out their faith haven't changed; they just got more complicated. Kids now need to *initiate* expressing their faith during the school day. By removing the school sponsorship of these religious activities, our kids are now set up to learn how to be intentionally proactive in exercising their rights and practicing their faith. Some might look at these Supreme Court rulings as "lemons," but actually they are opportunities for our children to make sweet-tasting lemonade with deep-rooted faith. This can be a positive step toward strengthening their faith in their spiritual journeys. When things are harder, our kids' faith roots have the opportunity to go deeper.

BE INTENTIONALLY PROACTIVE

Your kids aren't the only ones who have opportunities to be intentionally proactive in exercising their religious liberties in the public-school environment. You do too! Did you know that your child can participate in Bible study *during* public-school hours?

And it's protected by the Constitution. Are you surprised? Most parents are, and I was too.

In the following chapters, we'll look at three unique spaces afforded by the Constitution for your child to study the Bible at public school: *before- and after-school Bible clubs*, *Bible-literacy classes*, and *released-time Bible programs*. Bible clubs and programs have been around for years. If they're already present at your public school, all you need to do is find them and enroll your child. If they're not present yet, you could help get them started.

Here's the bottom line: Think about which of these Bible-study opportunities fits your child best, then be intentionally proactive about signing your child up and helping them get in the game.

"I Have Really Seen Him Grow!"

A mom was excited her son had started reading the Bible as a result of his participation in a released-time Bible class offered at his public school. She said, "I have really seen him grow! Yesterday I was feeling a bit sad, and he brought over his Bible, bookmarked with verses pertaining to sadness. Then he read those wonderful passages aloud to me. I was so encouraged!"

CHAPTER 7

BEFORE- AND AFTER-SCHOOL BIBLE CLUBS

Lisa was a guidance counselor at a public school. She was a faithful Christian and had a deep desire to be a positive influence on her students and colleagues. When she saw parents from her school initiate a Bible club after school hours, she was thrilled.

"One day a little girl had a big smile on her face as she walked into my counseling office," Lisa said. "I asked her why she was so happy. This little girl shared that she was excited to attend the new Bible club because her family didn't attend church." Then she said something that Lisa (and I) would never forget: "I go to church every night during the week too!" Lisa dove deeper with her questions and quickly discovered that every night, this little girl *walked* to a different church within a mile radius of her home because she was so hungry to learn more about the God of the Bible. It warmed Lisa's heart, and mine, to see how an after-school Bible club was impacting a young child's life for Christ.

A GROWING HUNGER

Like the little girl at Lisa's school, there is a growing hunger in kids for the truth found in the Word of God. Though many are looking at the next generation and assuming all is lost, the results of a survey conducted in 2022 by the Barna Group tell a different story:

> Though religious affiliation and church attendance continue to decline [in America], spiritual openness and curiosity are on the rise. Across every generation, in fact, we see an unprecedented desire to grow spiritually, a belief in a spiritual/supernatural dimension and a belief in God or a higher power.[1]

Those of us who pray and long for spiritual revival in our country should rejoice over the statistics from the Barna survey.[2] The spiritual climate of our country *has* changed and softened. Though the reasons for this change vary as greatly as the people themselves, one thing is certain: People from all walks of life are seeking spiritual truth. The despiritualizing of our public spaces, public squares, and public schools has only accentuated our desire as human beings for spiritual things. Though the Barna study doesn't specifically focus on those seeking Christ, around 75 percent of US adults, from Boomers to Gen Z, describe a spiritual hunger inside them.[3] And this is really good news.

We can only surmise that what the enemy intends for the deconstruction and dismantling of faith (whether in God or any higher power), God is using to draw people to Himself. Though public schools are now secular institutions by design, spiritual needs have not diminished. The bottom line is this: Our kids and their families are looking for the God of the Bible.

Even more exciting, the God of the Bible is pursuing them. And we have the privilege of pointing them to the only One who can satisfy their thirst: Jesus Christ.

Let's explore the first option available to families that brings the Word of God back into public schools: Bible clubs. Remember, the most important discipleship and Bible training happens in your home, but having invested adults, kids, and Christian peers studying the Word of God together also plays an essential role in the spiritual development of our children.

WHAT ARE BEFORE- AND AFTER-SCHOOL BIBLE CLUBS?

The US Department of Education views before- and after-school clubs as curricular or noncurricular student groups.[4] They're essentially small communities where students are welcomed and given the chance to participate in a shared activity or learning environment to further their educational, social, emotional, and/or spiritual growth. These clubs meet outside allotted instructional hours. Bible clubs specifically center around learning the Bible and are considered noncurricular and *devotional* in nature. *Devotional* in this context means that the club is focused on the spiritual growth and development of students and is not purely educational.

In America, Bible clubs have a long, rich history of providing religious instruction to children attending public school. As early as the 1920s, clubs were meeting before and after school hours. They lasted one hour to several hours and were administered by community or church volunteers rather than school staff. This new movement quickly spread across the United States.

Jesse Irvin Overholtzer was a preacher from California whom God used to pioneer a revolutionary movement. The prevailing thought in the late 1880s was that children weren't old enough to accept Christ as their Savior. In fact, his own mother told him at the age of twelve that he was too young to profess true faith in Christ. Later in life, as a pastor, Overholtzer was gripped by a thought-provoking quote he heard from renowned nineteenth-century theologian Charles Spurgeon: "A child of five, if properly instructed, can as truly believe and be regenerated as an adult."[5]

To test Spurgeon's theory, Overholtzer started a pilot after-school Bible club, called Good News Club, at the local public school. Within the first few months, twenty children accepted Christ as their Savior. Yet Overholtzer remained skeptical. Was this effort really making a difference? His mind changed, however, when he saw the spiritual impact of children's faith on Good News Club families. He was amazed when the mother of children who had given their lives to Christ at the Bible club walked up the church aisle and received salvation for herself. Overholtzer politely asked her why she decided to give her life to Jesus. She told him that it was the changed lives of her two little girls.

In 1937, fueled by the words of Spurgeon and Matthew 18:14, which says, "It is not the will of my Father who is in heaven that one of these little ones should perish," Overholtzer established the Bible-centered nonprofit organization Child Evangelism Fellowship (CEF). This interdenominational organization facilitates and administers Good News Clubs in public schools, as well as other ministries, serving hundreds of thousands of children throughout the United States and abroad.

In addition to Good News Clubs, there are many churches and organizations that share a passion for God's Word and are implementing their own independent school Bible clubs. Fellowship of Christian Athletes (FCA), which started in 1954, also provides before- and after-school Bible clubs for student athletes nationwide. Launched in 1966, these clubs are called *huddles*.[6] Although FCA primarily serves athletes, any student is welcome in their huddles.

Another Bible-centered nonprofit that facilitates Bible clubs throughout the country is KiDs Beach Club (KBC). Volunteers with KiDs Beach Clubs are passionate about teaching the Bible to elementary-aged kids through after-school clubs. Thankfully, anyone can initiate a club, providing a place that welcomes all public-school children to learn the Bible.

In case you're wondering, like Overholtzer, whether children are old enough to understand the gospel and give their lives to Christ, researchers continue to find Spurgeon's theory to be true. In fact, not only is it possible for children to make the life-changing decision to follow Christ; there is no more fertile time to sow the gospel in their hearts than in those early, formative years.

George Barna, through research he presents in his book *Raising Spiritual Champions: Nurturing Your Child's Heart, Mind and Soul*, discovered that our lifelong behaviors and beliefs are generally developed before we reach the teenage years. In particular, our moral foundations are generally in place by the time we reach the age of nine. And our response to the meaning and personal value of Jesus Christ's life, death, and resurrection is usually determined before we reach eighteen years of age. Though Jesus can transform any life at any age, children are especially fertile soil for the gospel between the ages of four and fourteen.[7] We must invest deeply in this season of their lives and spiritual development.

Although Bible clubs vary greatly, they are a worthy investment of time and resources. Whether held before or after school, a typical weekly Bible club for children from kindergarten to grade 12 can consist of a Bible lesson, worship songs, Bible memory verses, small-group discussion, activities, and games. Sometimes clubs are grade-specific, meaning one club per grade, and sometimes grades are combined in a club. Overall, Bible clubs aim to accomplish these goals:

- Build relationships and grow kids in their faith and knowledge of the Bible.
- Build godly character.
- Develop hearts of compassion for others.
- Provide a fun, encouraging environment where kids can share and discuss their beliefs.
- Help kids and their friends experience Jesus in their lives.

HOW IS THAT LEGAL ON SCHOOL PROPERTY?

Before- and after-school Bible clubs have no legal restrictions as long as they meet off campus and parents have given written permission for their children to attend. However, some Bible clubs are held on school property. So how can that be legal? This is a very good question, which you can have confidence in answering. Before- and after-school Bible clubs are legal on school property when they follow the federal Equal Access Act of 1984. Equal access means equal treatment for all noncurricular clubs.

The Equal Access Act (EAA) (20 U.S.C. 4071–74) requires public secondary schools that meet certain criteria to treat all student-initiated groups equally, regardless of the religious beliefs of the groups.[8] The EAA was adopted by Congress in 1984, and the US Supreme Court upheld its constitutionality in *Board of Education of Westside Community Schools v. Mergens* in 1990.[9]

Before your eyes glaze over, here's what this means for Bible clubs: When a school board opens school facilities to *any* student-led, noncurricular club, it must uniformly open its facilities to *all* student-led groups, including religious ones. So if there is even one noncurricular club allowed at a school, like a running club or a chess club, a Bible club must be permitted to meet at the facility for the school to stay in its legal lane.

While the Equal Access Act specifically mentions secondary schools (middle school and high school), based on the courts' interpretation of the US Constitution, equal access is required for religious community groups under the same terms as secular community groups. This means an elementary school Bible club led by community members can request permission to use space on a public-school campus, as long as other community groups, from bird-watching to bingo, are allowed the same access.

So if you're wondering, like I was, if equal access is still being protected by the courts—it is. Ironically, it hasn't been challenged in recent years. As parents, we can feel confident knowing that the Supreme Court has upheld before- and after-school noncurricular clubs on campus, including Bible clubs.

To find out whether a before- or after-school Bible club is offered at your child's school, start with the school website or inquire at the school office. Contacting the school's PTA (Parent Teacher Association) or the school board for information is a good idea as well. Once you find the name of the Bible club, talk to the main contact or submit an inquiry on the website about signing up your child. Then do it!

If no Bible club is offered at your child's school, make it a priority to find passionate leaders or organizations that make it easy to start one, like KiDs Beach Club, CEF, or FCA. If feasible, explore what it would look like to help launch a Bible club at the school. Remember, immersing your child in the Bible is key to spiritual growth! And you don't want your child to miss the many benefits of participating in a Bible club.

The Benefits of Bible Clubs

In addition to cultivating spiritual growth through studying the Bible and building relationships, before- and after-school Bible clubs can offer other key benefits:

1. *They provide additional enrichment and support.* Having a Bible club that provides positive enrichment for our children is a win. Club activities can sharpen their social skills and creativity, critical-thinking skills, reading and writing skills, and spiritual development. Our kids can also benefit from the support of positive Christian role models.

2. *They guard important instructional time.* Since Bible clubs meet before or after school hours, they don't conflict with the school schedule or interrupt instructional time. Consequently, students don't need to make up class work they might have missed.

3. *They're helpful for working parents.* In today's world, many working parents have job schedules that require them to either drop off their kids before school or pick them up an hour or so after school gets out. So they're looking for good things to fill their children's time. Before- and after-school Bible clubs can fill this time gap with a safe, positive, and godly alternative that blesses the family.

4. *They're a positive presence at school.* Though a little less obvious, a Bible club can make a lasting positive impression on

others who are in and around the school building when the club is meeting. People are observant and may be curious about what is going on. Administration, faculty, and the community can all be drawn to Christ when clubs are conducted in a winsome way. Others are exposed to the gospel simply because of a Bible club's presence.

The Challenges of Bible Clubs

I'm a big believer in knowing all the facts when evaluating an opportunity for my children, especially when it involves my family's schedule. Although there are many benefits for kids attending before- and after-school Bible clubs, there are three challenges you might want to consider when evaluating whether this type of club is a good fit for your child:

1. *No transportation to or from school.* Typically, before- and after-school Bible clubs are held on campus and don't provide transportation for your child to and from club meetings. So you'll need to arrange your schedule to transport your child or find a buddy your child can carpool with.
2. *Interference with extracurricular activities.* In today's culture, youth sports, music lessons, dance ensembles, and other noncurricular activities are often held after school. Bible club times may compete with these extracurricular activities, which can force your child to choose between Bible club and another activity.
3. *Attention-span challenges.* A shorter attention span early in the morning or after a long day of school is another challenge your child may encounter when participating in a

Bible club that meets before or after school. It's a good idea to evaluate which time of day works best so your child gets the maximum benefit out of the club.

The Impact of Bible Clubs

When children regularly participate in a Bible club that meets before or after school, what impact does it have on them and their families? Consider the following:

- *Decisions for Christ.* According to Child Evangelism Fellowship, there are over six thousand Good News Clubs in the United States that serve public-school students.[10] Each year, thousands of children who attend these clubs make decisions to follow Christ. And according to Jack Terrell, CEO and founder of KiDs Beach Club, more than ten thousand kids who have attended their clubs since 2006 have made decisions for Christ.[11]
- *Changed behavior.* Another positive outcome is the impact these clubs have on children's behavior, especially at school. To measure the educational impact, the University of Arizona conducted a study on the role the KiDs Beach Club after-school program plays in the academic lives of students at public elementary schools. The study found that when the students' social and emotional needs were met, they also developed interpersonal skills, emotional maturity, leadership skills, and an ability to show kindness and empathize with others. Public-school principals who participated in the research rated the program highly. In fact, one principal noted there were no behavior concerns for students who

attended the program, and positive behavior increased when more students participated. Another principal was quoted as saying, "KBC taught students how to be a friend, what it is like to stand up for someone, and how to become leaders."[12]

- *Changed lives.* "The impact of KiDs Beach Club on kids and families is amazing!" CEO Jack Terrell told me. He went on to share his favorite impact story, which involved a precious little girl:

> We give Bibles as a gift to every child who attends our KiDs Beach Club. One year, on the very day we gave her a Bible, a little girl trusted Christ as her Savior. It was beautiful! She was so excited. She took her Bible home and began reading it daily.
>
> One day, she was up in her room, and she suddenly yelled loudly through the house, "I found it! I found it!"
>
> Her mom was in the kitchen and heard her daughter yelling as her feet pounded hurriedly down the stairs. The little girl ran into the kitchen, out of breath, with her open Bible.
>
> Her mom asked her, "What did you find?"
>
> The girl beamed. "I found the prayer I prayed when I asked Jesus to be my forever friend a few weeks ago!" She showed her mom the words in her Bible.
>
> "That's incredible," her mom replied.
>
> Then the sweet girl looked at her mom and asked, "Mom, have *you* ever prayed that prayer?"

Her mom thought for a moment, then said, "No, I haven't."

The girl gently offered, "Mom, would you like to pray that prayer with me?"

Right there in the kitchen, the girl prayed with her mom and led her to Christ. As an added bonus, a few weeks later, they were both baptized together with big smiles on their faces.

KiDs Beach Club

Founded in 2006, KiDs Beach Club is a growing nonprofit organization in the United States that empowers Christ followers to share the message of Jesus with kids in grades 3–6 through after-school Bible clubs. KiDs Beach Club takes God's Word to public schools, connects kids to Christ, and puts Bibles in the hands of preteens during their most important years for spiritual development. The organization partners with churches to sponsor Beach Clubs in public schools and form relationships with kids and their families, school faculty, and others in the community. Beach Clubs present Scripture in a preteen-friendly way, aiming to get the Bible into the hands of kids so they can read it for themselves. In addition, KiDs Beach Club produces a weekly children's TV show that airs globally across broadcast, cable, satellite, and streaming outlets. For more information visit kidsbeachclub.org.

Before- and after-school Bible clubs are effective in filling the rising spiritual need our kids and their friends have to know God. Kids are more curious and open than ever before to learning about the God of the Bible, their Creator and Savior. As those who love the next generation, we can actively shape our children's learning environment by legally adding the Bible to it. And this is just the first of three ways. So go ahead and plug your children into either a before- or after-school Bible club. If your school doesn't have a club, explore how to start one. It might just be a fit for your children and provide the extra support they need to live out their faith in public school. It could change not only their lives but the lives of their friends and families as well.

"I Already Did It!"

A small group of boys were very excited about a salvation message their Bible leader was giving. Before the leader finished her message, one boy was already on his knees praying, eyes closed and lips moving quietly. When he finished, he looked up and declared, "I already did it! I asked Jesus into my heart!" He had been so eager to receive Christ that he didn't even wait for the invitation. Grinning from ear to ear, he boldly declared to his public-school friends that he was now a Christian too!

CHAPTER 8

BIBLE-LITERACY CLASSES

One gray, cloudy morning, I had a burning question on my mind as I drove to work. With years of experience working with young children as a children's-ministry director at a church and now the leader of a nonprofit, I clearly understood the value of teaching children the Bible through a devotional lens. But a friend had proposed a new idea: having kids study the Bible academically and objectively as a historical book, free from a particular religious philosophy.

As I drove, I wondered, *How would studying the Bible as a historical book help public-school kids educationally?* I had to admit that my friend's idea had merit. I'd spent time with Ken Ham, CEO of Answers in Genesis, who has often said of the Bible that they are not biblical *stories* we tell our children; they are biblical *accounts.*[1] Historians have proved that many biblical events and characters were real, backed up by cross-referenced, valid, historical data.

David was a real king of Israel, and the Israelites historically served as slaves of Egypt. There is also no viable historical dispute over the fact that Jesus was a real person who lived in Israel under Roman occupation. All of history is dated according to His life and death. He is even referenced in *Annals* (c. AD 116), the ancient writings of Roman historian and senator Tacitus.[2]

As usual, I was in a hurry as I pulled into my office parking lot. I was late for a staff meeting. Our team of stellar public-school ministry leaders were assembled around the conference table with essential mugs of steaming coffee in hand. Several were former public-school teachers with years of experience in the educational system. They were smiling and forgiving as I bustled through the doorway.

When I sat down in my chair, I immediately blurted out, "I heard from a friend that the Bible actually helps children grasp concepts taught in their public-school classes. I can see how studying the Bible academically as historical literature could help students understand history. But how can it help them grasp other subjects, like English, music, and art?"

I found out—a lot.

My question set off a flurry of discussion around the table. One particularly astute staff member took the lead in responding. "Kori, what if I told you that children are at a *disadvantage* academically if they have *not* studied the Bible?"

Wow. I had truly never thought of that. The implications of my question were surprising and far-reaching.

"Have you ever heard of the famous first line in the classic book *Moby Dick*?" she continued.

"Yes," I said. "'Call me Ishmael.'"

"How do you know the meaning behind the name *Ishmael*

without knowing the Bible?" she challenged. Good question. In case you aren't familiar with the biblical account of Ishmael, he was the banished son of Abraham born of his wife's handmaiden, Hagar. His name in literature often refers to being an exile or outcast.

Others around the table chimed in with practical examples. How could kids understand the compliment *You have the patience of Job* if they'd never read his story in the Old Testament? Like kernels of corn popping randomly, everyone started calling out names of works of classic literature interwoven with Bible references:

- *The Odyssey* and *The Iliad* by Homer
- *Hamlet* by Shakespeare
- *Oliver Twist* by Charles Dickens
- *Lord of the Flies* by William Golding
- *Paradise Lost* by John Milton
- *A Christmas Carol* by Charles Dickens
- *Inferno* by Dante Alighieri
- *The Pilgrim's Progress* by John Bunyan

I was convinced. I learned that morning that the Bible not only gives our kids spiritual context and meaning; its pages also provide educational context and meaning to deepen their public-school learning experience. If our children aren't studying the Bible on a devotional level or, at the very least, an academic level, they are at a disadvantage educationally. Armed with Bible knowledge, they're able to understand history, literature, music, and art through the lens of this rich book. The knowledge and context the Bible provides is essential for studying and understanding so much of what our education system teaches.

BIBLICAL INFLUENCE IN MUSIC

According to Dr. Sarah Grace Shewbert, former professor at Concordia University in Portland, Oregon, the Bible has played a significant role in the creation and performance of music in America since colonial times. Dr. Shewbert shares,

> Psalms, hymns, and spiritual songs were imported from Europe and newly created on American shores. Singing schools were established with the expressed purpose of enabling each and every churchgoer to participate fully in religious music-making.
>
> Classical music was also an important force in American community and church life. The Handel and Haydn Society, founded in 1815 in Boston, is America's oldest continuously performing arts organization. Two of their first major presentations were of Handel's *Messiah* and Haydn's *The Creation*, both of which are based on biblical texts.
>
> Later, musical themes from Handel's *Messiah* were used in the hymn tune "Antioch" . . . , which is now best known as the Christmas carol, "Joy to the World." In 1907, the hymn "Joyful, Joyful, We Adore Thee" was set to a melody from Beethoven's Ninth Symphony.[3]

Shewbert also points out other popular musicians who have directly quoted the Bible. They include Pete Seeger from the 1960s band the Byrds, who wrote "Turn! Turn! Turn!" The lyrics of this song were drawn from Ecclesiastes 3:1-8. Likewise, "40" by U2 from the 1983 album *War* is a spin-off of Psalm 40. In 2015, the band Twenty One Pilots released the song "Hometown" as part of the album *Blurryface*, which makes many Bible references, including to Joshua 24:14; Ezekiel 37:1-14; and Acts 2:3. Even modern music icon Taylor Swift, whose lyrics and ideology sometimes show disdain for the Christian faith, makes reference to biblical values, the Holy Ghost, and prayer in her *Tortured Poets Department* album.[4] If our children don't know the biblical references or values conveyed in musical works, they won't be able to fully understand what the artists are trying to communicate.

BIBLICAL INFLUENCE IN ART

Early followers of Jesus used simple drawings of a cross, an anchor, or a fish to identify themselves as Christians after His death. For example, when the Romans were persecuting followers of Christ, one believer might trace half of a fish in the dirt with his toe, and another believer would trace the other half of the fish to identify themselves as Christians. Artists today continue to use biblical symbols of Christianity, including the cross and the fish, not just as an expression of faith, but to communicate a variety of religious and secular messages.[5]

Globally, Christian churches house astoundingly beautiful art. Much of this art depicts the life of Christ or the lives of saints through magnificent sculptures and paintings. Throughout history, the purpose of art was almost exclusively instructional or decorative to help people connect with the divine.

Leonardo da Vinci's *The Last Supper*, Michelangelo's *David*, and sculptor Gheorghe Leonida's work on *Christ the Redeemer*, a towering statue in Rio de Janeiro, Brazil, depicting Jesus Christ with outstretched arms, were all inspired by the Bible. Without knowledge of the Bible, children miss the message these artists sought to communicate about God.

BIBLE ENGAGEMENT IS DECLINING

For years my friend Lee has prayed with her daughters for their classmates. When they were in early elementary school, Lee and the girls decided to invite their school friends over for a Christmas party. They created invitations for the girls to hand-deliver at school and started preparing for the Friday-afternoon event. Lee made sure the moms were invited as well, and she carefully spelled out what the activities would include: a Christmas craft, sugar-cookie decorating, reading the original Christmas story from the Bible, and Christmas carols. The RSVPs rolled in, and Lee had to expand the party space in their home to accommodate more girls and moms.

Lee and the girls had an eager captive audience and found that after an hour of crafting and cookie decorating, everyone was in the mood for a few moments by their Christmas tree. As Lee finished the Bible reading from Luke 2, she closed the illustrated Bible and said, "That's what Christmas is all about."

A young girl looked up at her and said, "I know Jesus died on a cross."

Lee replied, "That's right. Jesus did die on a cross, but what happened on Easter?"

The girl stared at her and said, "I don't know."

Lee tried again. "What is Easter all about?"

Only Lee's girls and a few of the moms had any idea.

Unfortunately, Lee's story about her children's classmates isn't unusual. This generation of kids and many of their parents are unfamiliar with even the most basic Bible stories—stories that American and school holidays are built around. But why?

In its 2024 *State of the Bible* report, the American Bible Society (ABS) stated that 57 percent of US adults (151 million) are Bible disengaged. The report also showed that at 38 percent, or 99 million adults, fewer Americans than ever are Bible users.[6] According to ABS, "Bible Users are individuals who interact with the Bible on their own at least three times a year."[7] Consequently, this disengagement trend trickles down to our children. If kids aren't learning about the Bible, they are missing crucial information and context for much of what they're learning in school history, classic and modern literature, music, and art. And that's alarming.

Our Founding Fathers, as well as the fathers of American education, knew the Word of God was foundational for true education. The Dunham Bible Museum preserved the following for us:

> Education in the earliest [American] colleges was also founded on the Bible. College students at Harvard and Yale were required to read the Scriptures twice daily, and be able to give an account of their reading. Early Harvard rules stated, "[T]he only foundation of all knowledge and learning" [is] Jesus Christ.[8]

Whether or not children are able to engage with the Bible devotionally, when it comes to public school, Bible-literacy classes are one way to fill their *educational* gap. These classes help children deepen their understanding and appreciation of how vital this book is not only for our history and culture but also for opening the doors of faith.

WHAT ARE BIBLE-LITERACY CLASSES?

Bible-literacy classes are elective classes that teach the Bible from the perspective of literature, history, or its cultural impact. Like any other academic course, these classes are taught mostly on school property during school hours or virtually on a digital device. However, they must be exclusively academic, with no faith component. Curriculum must have a viewpoint-neutral perspective and be nondevotional in nature.

Several Bible-literacy curricula for public high schools have gained traction in the last few decades in the United States. Essentials in Education, started in 2005 through the Bible Literacy Project, created "instructional resources to assist school districts in implementing a Bible course in public schools. It ensured the content of the Bible would be taught academically and objectively—and not from a particular religious philosophy."[9]

Another organization that has moved the needle in this area is the National Council on Bible Curriculum in Public Schools. It also has a neutral-view product and has helped implement their Bible curriculum in thirty-five hundred high schools in more than forty states throughout the country.[10] BibLit, based in Tennessee, has taken a new approach to Bible literacy by offering online Bible-literacy classes for high school students. They have several different courses to pick from and serve students online with excellence.

The Museum of the Bible, located in Washington, DC, has also released a high school curriculum to promote Bible literacy, titled *The Bible's Influence on Western Civilization*. The curriculum focuses on the manifestation of a biblical story or theme in Western culture. With chapters on the creation account, Elijah, John the Baptist, and Jesus' miracle stories, students learn one of these narratives in each lesson and how it is embedded in culture through film, painting, music, sculpture, and literature.

BibLit

BibLit (Bible Literature Online) is an organization that uses "online, teacher-led, and viewpoint-neutral courses to help students discover the history, ideas, and cultural legacy of the Bible." They offer for-credit online courses that are engaging and interactive, taking high school students "through the sweep of history to discover ancient Bible literature and its impact on modern ideas and works of art."[11] The constitutionally compliant courses "enable students to acquire an understanding, fluency with, and appreciation of the Bible's major ideas, historical [and] geographical contexts, literary forms, and its impact on later cultures, societies, and religions."[12] Students not only benefit from teacher-facilitated courses and student-support specialists, but they can also earn full elective credits while enjoying flexible scheduling. BibLit is meeting a growing online need in our public-education system. For more information, visit biblit.org.

HOW IS BIBLE TEACHING LEGAL IN PUBLIC SCHOOLS?

You may be wondering how it's legal for public schools to teach about the Bible and religion. Me too! When we look back at the First Amendment, we read that "Congress shall make no law respecting an establishment of religion."[13] This means our public schools cannot engage in teaching that would be considered evangelistic or encourage students to think a certain way about any particular religion. That would constitute establishing a religion. However, teaching *about* different religions and historical events and figures is part of a well-rounded educational curriculum.

The US Department of Education explains it like this:

> Public schools may not provide religious instruction, but they may teach *about* religion. For example,

> philosophical questions concerning religion, the history of religion, comparative religion, the Bible (or other religious teachings) as literature, and the role of religion in the history of the United States and other countries all are permissible public school subjects. Similarly, it is permissible to consider religious influences on philosophy, art, music, literature, and social studies.[14]

Therefore, it's permissible to teach children about the Israelites' captivity in Egypt from a purely historical and factual perspective as part of an Egyptian-studies class.

The Big Influence of the Bible

The Museum of the Bible is a global, innovative educational institution that invites all people to engage with the transformative power of the Bible. I have enjoyed visiting several times, where interactive exhibits and cutting-edge technology immersed me in its impact, narrative, and history.

Passionate about helping young people engage with Scripture, the museum released a high school textbook titled *The Bible's Influence on Western Civilization*. This curriculum guides students through history, art, music, literature, and language, showing how the Bible has shaped creative expression across centuries and cultures. Students discover that biblical stories have inspired music from Mozart to Bob Dylan to U2 as well as films like *The Matrix*. Rich with historical examples and images, the textbook helps students trace connections across societies—especially America's—and reveals how the world's most widely read book continues to spark creativity and cultural dialogue today.

For more information, visit museumofthebible.com.

The Benefits of Bible-Literacy Classes

As we discussed earlier, Bible-literacy classes can teach children how the Bible has impacted history, music, systems of government, politics, arts, and morals. But Bible-literacy classes offer a few more benefits for public-school children:

- *They introduce kids to the Bible.* Bible-literacy classes, at their core, introduce children to the Bible through an academic lens, which is especially beneficial for those who have never been exposed to this rich book.
- *They highlight the Bible's value academically.* These classes allow children to see the value of learning the Bible in an educational context, not just a religious one. Studying the Bible for its literary and cultural value can equip children with a variety of critical-thinking skills. It can be challenging for kids to read the Bible, so studying it can help them formulate questions with other students.
- *They allow for-credit courses.* Some high schools and colleges allow for-credit Bible-literacy classes in humanities, literature, or history. Dual-credit courses are also available in some school districts to benefit students.

The Challenges of Teaching the Bible in Public Schools

Not everyone agrees that the Bible should be taught in public school. Disagreement begins with the controversy over which Bible version to use. Furthermore, critics of Bible-literacy classes assert that teachers view the text through their own worldview lens and will inevitably teach the material, even innocently, based on their personal biases. History is complex and messy. This includes biblical history. Knowingly or unknowingly, teachers could make religious claims in either direction and violate the First Amendment Establishment Clause.[15]

Of the three unique spaces where the Bible fits into the public-school experience, Bible-literacy classes have the most challenges. Here are a few more:

- *They rely on public-school administrators for approval.* School administrators need to see the value in offering a Bible-literacy class at their child's public school and approve the goals. Given the many curriculum requirements for faculty and students, these classes don't always take a high priority in their strategic plan for the school year.
- *They require additional funding for teachers.* Not only do school administrators need to approve Bible-literacy classes, but school districts also need to have the additional funding set aside for teachers who will be implementing the program. With so many things competing for budgetary dollars, funding for these classes can be hard to find.
- *They present only facts, not faith.* Although learning about the Bible at any level is beneficial, learning just the facts can leave a gap in your child's spiritual development. Supplemental teaching is needed. Children still need to hear the gospel and study the Bible devotionally to experience healthy spiritual growth.

The Impact of Bible-Literacy Classes

When public schools offer Bible-literacy classes either in person or virtually, it sparks conversation about the Bible, arguably the most important book in history; cultivates critical-thinking skills; and promotes educational development. Its impact is seen through the number of students who have completed the classes. While the impact of studying the Bible is generally measured by lives changed, when gauging the impact of Bible-literacy classes that have a viewpoint-neutral requirement, we must evaluate the number of students served instead. Here are some attendance results Bible-literacy organizations reported in 2024:

- The Bible Literacy Project reports that "to date, 650 schools and 150,000 students in 45 states have been taught the material in [their] Bible literacy course."[16]
- According to the National Council on Bible Curriculum in Public Schools, 3,500 public high schools in 41 states are currently using their Bible curriculum, and more than 650,000 students in the United States have taken the course.[17]
- BibLit shares on its website that "over 400 students have earned credit for the course in four public school districts," and demand for these classes is growing.[18]

The answer to my original burning question, "How would studying the Bible as a historical book help public-school kids educationally?" opened my eyes to a new way of looking at this ancient book. Not only does it give our kids spiritual context and meaning, but it also deepens their educational context. The Bible greatly enriches meaning in subjects like history, English, art, and music. The truth is, if our children are not taught the Bible, they're not only at a spiritual disadvantage but are at an educational disadvantage as well.

Fortunately, according to John Farquhar Plake, American Bible Society chief program officer and *State of the Bible* editor in chief, "Last year, 50 percent of Gen Z adults (ages 18–27) agreed that the message of the Bible has transformed their lives. This year, that number rose to 54 percent. If this trend continues, we have good reason for hope."[19]

Friend, from where I sit, this is very good news.

"I Never Knew . . ."

After learning about God, Jesus, and the Bible, a third-grade boy shared, "I never knew *any* of that before!" Then he added that the best thing he learned was that "God made me."

CHAPTER 9

RELEASED-TIME BIBLE PROGRAMS

The large church hall echoed and hummed with excitement and the chatter of third graders. Eager volunteers with bright-blue T-shirts weaved their way through the large group of children, guiding them to their seats. Their parents had signed them up to attend an off-campus released-time Bible program, called Bible2School, during their lunch and recess periods every Wednesday. The day had finally arrived!

I was a new volunteer small group leader learning the ropes when I met Gabriel. He was an adorable, blonde, curly-haired little boy in my group with light-blue eyes and a light-up-the-sky smile. Gabriel lived with his grandmother in the city. He didn't seem to know much about God. The biblical accounts of the life of King David, Daniel, and even Jesus seemed brand-new to him. But Gabriel eagerly attended the Bible2School program every week to learn more.

One Wednesday, as a roomful of kids were eating their lunches, one teacher was sharing the message of salvation. In child-friendly terms, she explained to the children how they could ask Jesus into their lives forever, using the Bible2School CBA Cross acronym:

> Confess that you have sinned and made bad choices.
> Believe that Jesus died for the forgiveness of your sins.
> Ask God to forgive your sins and ask Him to be part of your life forever.

The teacher gave the children time to consider this invitation and pray with her if they desired. Gabriel stopped, folded his hands, bowed his head, and silently prayed. When he was finished, he looked up and caught my eye with a big grin on his face.

I said, "Gabriel, did you ask Jesus to come into your life forever?"

He happily replied, "Yes, I did." And then he said something I will *never* forget. He drew his eyebrows together thoughtfully and added, "I've always wanted to know how to get to heaven, but no one ever told me."

My breath caught. Gabriel's innocent statement instantly pulled at my heart. There are so many kids in America who have never heard the gospel. So many who don't know the life-transforming, eternity-shaping truth that Jesus loves them. Some of them will never step foot in a church, and this might be the only opportunity they get to hear about God.

Before- and after-school Bible clubs and Bible-literacy classes are both viable options that address the rising hunger students have for learning about spiritual matters. In this chapter, we'll explore a third unique space for the Bible in public school: released-time Bible programs. I firmly believe this option outshines the other two because it immerses our children in the Bible with excellence.

Released-time Bible programs are designed to share the gospel with children devotionally, strengthen their faith, and provide convenience for families. Free elective programs like this also assist parents in meeting spiritual goals for their kids.

I'm partial to this option because I'm the CEO of Bible2School, the dynamic released-time Bible program I mentioned at the beginning of this chapter. A released-time Bible program could be a great fit for your kids as you seek to fill them up with God's Holy Word during their school week. Let's explore what sets these programs apart from the others.

WHAT ARE RELEASED-TIME BIBLE PROGRAMS?

A released-time Bible program offers religious instruction for students at an off-campus location during public-school hours. These programs are usually offered by local organizations or churches. In some states, children have the right to participate in released-time Bible programs with parental permission. In other states, schools have discretion to excuse students from school to attend a released-time program. While this right has been secured in most school districts, it's still an ongoing topic of discussion for parents.

In 1914, Dr. William Wirt, an innovative educator and superintendent of the Gary, Indiana, public schools, implemented the first released-time Bible program.[1] These programs quickly gained in popularity and spread around the country. When their legality was initially challenged in the 1940s, the US Supreme Court ruled in *McCollum v. Board of Education* (1948) that a released-time Bible program in Champaign, Illinois, had violated the Establishment Clause of the First Amendment because religious instruction took place on campus during school hours.[2] But the tide turned in 1952 when the Supreme Court upheld the New York appeals-court ruling in *Zorach v. Clauson*, which stated that the released-time program in New York City public schools did *not* violate the First Amendment, since it involved "neither religious instruction in public schools nor the expenditure of public funds."[3]

The main objective of released-time Bible programs is offering off-campus Bible instruction to public-school students, especially those who aren't able to attend church. Students from kindergarten to grade 12 can walk or be bused to a nearby church or partner location *during* school hours to participate in a released-time program. Trained, caring volunteers and staff engage them in biblical teaching, activities, prayer, and worship. Programs last anywhere from half an hour to an hour, typically once a week for a set period of time during the school year. Kids enjoy engaging with the Bible through interactive games, reenacting Bible stories, working on fun crafts, watching inspiring videos, and participating in small-group activities that emphasize and apply the Bible lesson to their lives.

Released-time Bible programs have historically been hosted by local, independent community groups and churches. However, the number of new programs has rapidly increased thanks to the efforts of national organizations like Bible2School and LifeWise Academy.

Bible2School

Bible2School equips communities across the nation to provide free, elective released-time Bible programs to elementary-aged, public-school children *during* their school day. We believe that *every* child needs to hear biblical truth, so our goal is to make it easy and convenient for parents.

Bible2School is unique from other programs in the way we intentionally engage children with the Bible. In small groups, kids discuss the Bible lesson with their leader and answer a "Think About It" question, which allows them to explore the ideas presented during the lesson and make connections to their own faith journeys. Examples of these spiritual questions are "How can you forgive others?" and "How can you fully rely on God?"

With the help of the Holy Spirit, dots are connected from their heads to their hearts. Bible2School "gives children a safe place to ask spiritual questions and process how to apply biblical truth to their everyday lives."[4] And God uses these intentional relationships to change lives.

Bible2School's vision is that "every public school in our nation would have a dynamic Bible program taught during their school day as allowed by national released time court rulings."[5]

For more information, visit bible2school.com.

HOW ARE THESE PROGRAMS LEGAL?

Many people ask how "releasing" children from public school to learn from the Bible during the school day is legal in the United States. I know I did. In the early 1900s, since religious instruction wasn't included in public-school education, leaders recognized that local communities could take on this task. The federal released-time provision was a great solution. One thing to note is that released-time programs are open to *all* religions, not just the Christian religion. Released-time Bible programs focus on devotional teaching, so the curriculum is designed for spiritual growth rather than instruction in Bible history.

Over the years, the legality of the program has been supported by federal court rulings, including the *Zorach v. Clauson* ruling mentioned earlier. To be legal, released-time Bible programs must adhere to three requirements:

1. *They need to be held off-site.* The program takes place off school property. It cannot be held anywhere on public-school grounds, including the parking lot.
2. *To attend classes, students need permission from their parents or guardians.* Parental permission is required for a child to participate in the program. Most programs request a signed permission form to fulfill this requirement.
3. *No tax dollars can be used.* Not one cent of taxpayer funds can be used in implementing or sustaining a program, including something as small as using the school copier (which costs money).

Now that we've settled the issue of legality, let's consider the benefits, challenges, and impact of released-time Bible programs.

The Benefits

Of the three unique spaces where the Bible can be taught in public school, released-time Bible programs are the least known and yet potentially the most impactful.

As CEO of Bible2School, I've witnessed great benefits bubble to the top and turn into blessings for students and families through these programs:

- *Convenience for families.* Busy parents don't have to worry about providing transportation for their children to participate in the program. Since classes take place during school hours, parents don't have to drop their kids off before school or pick them up after school. Students may walk to the nearby church or partner location where the classes are being held, or the program sponsors provide transportation.
- *Solid biblical teaching.* Parents can trust that the solid biblical teaching and positive biblical values their children receive from released-time programs will equip them for life.
- *Consistent investment in spiritual growth.* Regular attendance, which is sometimes lacking in before- and after-school programs, translates into a consistent investment in spiritual growth. Caring leaders deepen relationships with kids as they teach about Jesus and become positive role models in their lives.
- *Opens doors to spiritually unconnected friends.* It often isn't easy for children to invite their spiritually unconnected friends to a weekend church service. But inviting a friend to a released-time Bible program during the school week is easy and convenient. According to a Bible2School parent survey, "16% of children attended [a released-time program] because a friend invited them." Remarkably, "17% of the children came because their parents were invited by other parents to check out the program and its benefits."[6]

Released-time Bible programs remove many barriers for parents who want to provide their children with spiritual enrichment on a weekly basis. This program is certainly worth investigating.

The Challenges

The challenges you might encounter if your child attends a released-time Bible program are minimal but worth reviewing:

- *Potential for missed instructional time.* Since classes meet off campus once a week during school hours, your child could miss instructional time and need to make up class work. Program leaders and parents coordinate with schools to ensure that children who attend these classes have the educational support they need. Some released-time programs even schedule their classes over lunch or during free periods to minimize the potential for missed instruction time.
- *Condensed program time.* Because transporting children off-site reduces learning time, classes tend to be shorter, around thirty to forty-five minutes, compared to Sunday-school classes, which are typically sixty to ninety minutes. Released-time Bible curriculum is often condensed into essential biblical accounts and truths to maximize impact.
- *Possible safety concerns.* Transportation safety and off-site building safety are two concerns to consider before enrolling your child in a released-time Bible program. Make sure you thoroughly understand and are comfortable with the program's safety policies before entrusting your child to the care and oversight of others.

The Impact

The impact of released-time Bible programs is far-reaching. These programs satisfy a spiritual hunger in public-school kids. Not only do parents see positive changes in their kids, but educators and community members also witness the transformation of children's lives by the Word of God. Here are a few key statistics and comments on the impact of released-time Bible programs:

- Ninety percent of educators agreed that their school and students benefit from the LifeWise released-time program.[7] School attendance improved, and both in-school and out-of-school suspensions decreased. One educator shared, "You can tell which students attend [a released-time program]. Those kids have become kinder and more courteous. I've seen a change in them when they come back to school."
- Seventeen percent of parents reported that they began attending church because their child was participating in a released-time Bible program.[8] One mom hugged me tight after a church service and shared that her daughter begged her to take her to church after attending a released-time program. It was the catalyst that got her whole family to start attending church. "We will never be the same," she told me through her tears.
- Approximately 60 percent of the children who register for a Bible2School program each year don't regularly attend church services or have a working knowledge of spiritual things.[9] These kids are now aware of God's incredible love, plan, and purpose for them.

MY TABLE FULL OF GIRLS

One Wednesday before Easter, I was volunteering as a small-group leader for a Bible2School program. Five sweet third-grade girls, who had no church background, sat in a circle around my table. We had just watched the first part of a three-part movie about Jesus. I asked the girls if they had any questions about the movie so far.

One little girl shyly raised her hand and asked tentatively, "What was Jesus doing with that girl who was sleeping?" (The girl in the movie was Jairus's daughter from Mark 5:21-24, 35-42.)

I told her, "Honey, she wasn't sleeping. She was dead, and Jesus raised her to life."

The girls gasped, and all eyes around the table got big.

I continued, "It gets even better than that. In a few weeks, you'll see Jesus suffering and dying for our sins in our place. But God raised Him from the dead so we could be with Him in heaven forever!"

Then around that table, something amazing happened. In the middle of the week, in the middle of a school day, four of the five little girls bowed their heads and asked Jesus into their lives forever. Tears of joy flooded my eyes. I couldn't imagine being anywhere else. What a gift to introduce these sweet girls to Jesus and His power.

A GROWING MOVEMENT

Demand is increasing for released-time Bible programs among public-school parents. The convenience of these programs and their effectiveness in meeting the spiritual needs of our children is undeniable. Some of the leading organizations that equip communities to implement released-time Bible programs have reported a wave of growth. The number of children attending Bible2School has grown by over 400 percent in the last few years.[10] And

LifeWise Academy, which operates a rapidly growing released-time Bible program, reports that the number of schools they serve has doubled in the last two years.[11] Joel Penton, founder and CEO of LifeWise Academy, recently told me the following in an email:

> Every day we see the impact of unleashing the Word of God into the lives of kids. Attitudes and behavior improve, but more importantly, children are being spiritually transformed by the love of God! Kids and their families are reconnecting with churches[,] and communities are being changed![12]

Busy parents with jam-packed calendars are recognizing that a released-time Bible program is a viable solution for their children. According to a study by Utah State University, parents understand that children do better in school when they participate in a religious program on a regular basis.[13] They actually do better in life. Mental, emotional, and behavioral problems decrease when kids get to know the God who made them, loves them, and has a beautiful plan and purpose for their lives through the saving power of Jesus.

AN INVITATION TO SHAPE YOUR CHILD'S LEARNING ENVIRONMENT

All three unique spaces—before- and after-school Bible clubs, Bible-literacy classes, and released-time Bible programs—allow the Bible to fit into public schools. And each of these options is supported by the Constitution and upheld by the Supreme Court. Surprisingly, they have been legal for many years. They help our kids grow in their faith and deepen their learning experiences through an educational context, and they consistently disciple and equip our children to live out their faith wherever they are in their busy lives.

As parents, we aren't bystanders in our children's learning experiences in public school. God has provided these three unique spaces as opportunities to actively shape our children's learning environment and make sure the Bible is included in it.

I have an important question for you: Which of these three spaces is a fit for your children?

Only you can discern which is best.

I invite you to get off the bleachers. You have the power to immerse your children in the Bible. Get informed about their religious freedoms and sign them up for a Bible club, a Bible-literacy class, or a released-time Bible program that can help them engage with the Bible during the school week.

You'll also need to know how to partner and communicate well with your children's public schools, which can sound daunting. But don't worry. In the next chapter, I'll share what has worked well for me and scores of other parents. The goal is to help your children get in the game and live out their faith in public school. And together we'll accomplish that goal.

We'll begin by helping our kids pack their backpacks.

"I Didn't Know!"

"I didn't know who God was. I just knew He was associated with a cross in some way. I'm glad Bible2School exists, because I would have never accepted God into my life because I probably never would have heard about Him."

IVY, FIFTH GRADER IN PUBLIC SCHOOL

PART FOUR

Preparing Your Kids to Get in the Game

CHAPTER 10

PREPARING VERSUS PROTECTING

Years ago I went to visit a friend from college I hadn't seen in a long time. She greeted me at the front door with a big smile and her precious toddler perched on her hip. This little guy had big brown eyes and dark curly hair. He was energetic and just learning how to walk.

As I entered my friend's house, I was shocked at what I saw before me. The room looked a bit like a fortified bunker from an old war movie. Big white pillows covered the entire space from my knees down, and little tunnels had been created for a toddler to walk through. Pillows were literally everywhere. They were on the floor propped up against every wall, every stick of furniture, every doorframe, and every appliance. As I carefully found my way to her sofa, I marveled at the giant padded toddler maze before me.

I asked her, "Why all the pillows?"

"They're to protect my child as he learns to walk," she replied.

It's natural to want to protect our children. It *feels* scary for us to let them take steps on their own. There is risk involved as they're learning to walk, both physically and metaphorically. While we would love to protect them from every potential harm, we can't. In fact, it would be impossible. There just aren't enough pillows in the world. Cushioning their path from all harm isn't God's plan for our kids, and it can't be our plan either. Ultimately, trying to control their environment will backfire or burn us out. And it won't help our kids learn to walk confidently in their faith.

Every parent must prayerfully decide the best method for educating their child. This decision needs to be made from a place of wisdom, not fear. Each family and each child has different needs and capabilities. There is no one-size-fits-all schooling method. Although many Christian parents choose to homeschool or send their children to private school, a majority of Christian parents in America still send their children to a public school. According to the Pew Research Center, public-school enrollment in 2021 was 83 percent, compared with 10 percent and 7 percent, respectively, for private schools and charter schools.[1] The concern I hear most often was vocalized in a question that a reader asked me in a *Washington Times* Higher Ground opinion column I contribute to:

> My children are . . . in the public school system. Homeschooling isn't currently financially viable for my family. How can I best protect my child from harmful cultural elements while still keeping them in the public system?[2]

Can't you hear the love and concern in this mother's all-too-common question? I can, and I know that concern myself. When we decide to send our children to public school, there is often uncertainty that lingers, even for believers, about their physical and spiritual safety. In an age where so many protections are afforded to our children—helmets when riding a bike, crossing guards for crossing a busy street—our first thought when faced with fear or danger is easily one of protection. We want to keep our kids away from ideologies that might damage their faith we are so diligently trying to nurture in them. This is natural.

But what if instead of asking how we can *protect* our children, we shift the paradigm and ask how we can *prepare* them? Preparing kids for the path ahead—equipped with a deep understanding of the love of God, wisdom in walking God's way, and joy in cultivating godly habits and relationships—*is* protection. There is nothing passive about the work required to prepare your children to stand on their own. Your first step is deciding to get in the game and embrace your role as the equipper for their road ahead.

I once heard a Navy SEAL say, "Always play offense. Prepare before you get there." The best way to protect your children from harmful cultural elements in the public-school system is preparation. Together we've explored the religious rights and freedoms your child maintains within school walls. If you've made it this far with me, you've seen that the constitutional rights of students to express their faith have been protected and upheld in courts around the nation. This knowledge acts as the base or foundation for preparing your children for what lies ahead. The next step is teaching them to recognize the prevailing culture messaging in their school environment.

LEARNING TO RECOGNIZE CULTURAL MESSAGING

The majority of public schools align with Judeo-Christian values when it comes to teaching students positive character traits. Kindness, respectfulness, obedience, honesty, integrity, and loving your neighbor are just a few examples of positive behavioral traits cultivated in a public-school environment. These universal traits are good for your child and the school because they help ensure an orderly, pleasant, and safe learning environment.

But there are other messages our children hear during their school day that aren't positive or good. Harmful cultural messaging that seeps into the public-school system not only fails to align with the Word of God but is often hostile to it.

One perspective that permeates our public-school system and has historically deep roots is *secular humanism.* We must recognize this worldview as the basis of our children's education in public school, with or without a teacher's knowledge. Simply put, secular humanism is atheism, "a lack of belief or a strong disbelief in the existence of a god or any gods."[3] It is a man-centered system of ethics that leaves God totally out of the picture. As theologian Francis Schaeffer observed, this system of belief embraces the view that man is "the measure of all things."[4] In essence, humanists believe that man is his own god.

This is not the religious neutrality required of public schools according to the Constitution. It is an education-shaping belief system.

Secular humanism has been around for a long time. It's believed that Anglican priests first used the phrase in the 1930s. In the 1940s, William Temple, the archbishop of Canterbury, warned that the "Christian tradition . . . was in danger of being undermined by a 'Secular Humanism' *which hoped to retain Christian values without Christian faith*" (emphasis added).[5]

The starting point of secular humanism is a denial or disbelief in the existence of a supreme being or god. This worldview claims, in the words of Carl Sagan, that "the cosmos [nature] is all that is or ever was or ever will be,"[6] and its theories for the existence of our universe rely solely on science. Secular humanists see themselves as beings that are the unintentional result of evolution.

Believe it or not, the US government recognizes secular humanism as a religion. In 2014, a federal district court in Oregon ruled that "Secular Humanism is a religion for Establishment Clause purposes."[7]

This, of course, is not at all the message of the Bible, which tells us that God is the Creator of the universe and the Author of life. The Bible also teaches that humankind is created in God's image and that He sovereignly rules over the earth and human matters. Humans are actually not in charge, and science can be misunderstood. Apart from God, we know nothing. Scripture is clear: "The fear of the LORD is the beginning of wisdom, and the knowledge of the Holy One is insight" (Proverbs 9:10).

So what do secular humanists claim that is contrary to the Word of God? And how has secular humanism found its way into our public schools disguised as truth?

Over the years, public schools have embedded a range of theories or philosophies in their curriculum and have, unfortunately, presented them as proven fact.

Consider the following secular-humanist claims and the clarity of Scripture in response:

Claims of Secular Humanism	What God's Word Says
The universe came into existence as a result of the "big bang" (the origin of the universe).	"In the beginning, God created the heavens and the earth" (Genesis 1:1).
Man evolved from apes (evolution).	"God created man in his own image" (Genesis 1:27).

Claims of Secular Humanism	What God's Word Says
There is no absolute right or wrong (moral relativism).	"Jesus said . . . , 'I am the way, and the truth, and the life. No one comes to the Father except through me'" (John 14:6).
Feelings determine whether you are a girl or a boy (gender ideology).	"Male and female [God] created them" (Genesis 1:27, NLT).
Follow your heart (emotionalism).	"The heart is deceitful above all things, and desperately sick; who can understand it?" (Jeremiah 17:9).

If you're shocked by this information, don't be. Satan is really good at serving up lies couched in enough truth to make us believe them. After all, secular humanism *does* encourage good morals. It is "a way of life, aiming at the maximum possible fulfilment, through the cultivation of ethical and creative living."[8] Yet theories and philosophies shift and morph with societal changes. This strategy is nothing new. Satan's deception is as old as time. He has always wanted humans to believe that we are the gods of ourselves.

Though secular humanism is poisonous, it need not deal a fatal blow to our children's faith. We must simply acknowledge that the enemy has a foothold in our children's lives and draw their attention to it. Parents often avoid or fail to clarify the truth for their children. This is easy to do because the deception begins subtly. Ignoring the problem can inhibit our children's ability to practice dealing with obstacles and harmful ideologies. We actually strengthen their walk with God when we teach them to identify things that don't align with God's Holy Word.

The prevailing theories and claims of secular humanism are

present throughout our culture. When we teach our children to recognize the deceptive messaging in their daily lives, they learn to identify these messages when we aren't with them at school. This is the best way to prepare and protect our children.

FILLING KIDS' BACKPACKS OF FAITH

Before I sent my firstborn off to kindergarten, I took my son shopping for important school supplies to fill his cool new navy-blue backpack. He loved his backpack so much that he wore it to the store. I laughed at his eagerness to begin his educational journey. But an empty backpack wouldn't get him very far in school. Just as I had thoughtfully and diligently packed his diaper bag with essentials from diapers to blankets to snacks when he was a baby, his faith backpack needed to be filled with essential supplies for his educational journey. The coolest binder, the brightest colored markers and crayons, and the best writing paper were all packed carefully. These supplies covered his educational needs, but what about supplies that would support his faith walk? I wondered what kinds of supplies he would need to walk confidently with God during his school day.

As I sat staring at the spot in our home where I always hugged my kids goodbye for the day, I vividly remember whispering prayers over them, reminding them (and me) of God's promised presence. I remember asking the Lord to reveal to my husband and me where the holes were in our parenting, and to protect and gird our children in the areas where we fell short. They were, after all, His children first.

For the remainder of this book, I'll share the essential backpack supplies I've found that will equip each of your children to live out their faith at school. I recommend you "pack" these seven essential faith supplies in their school backpacks with loving care:

- a water bottle (living water from God's Word)
- a notebook (God-confidence through prayer)
- a pencil case (a safe place for questions)
- a glue stick (to stick together as a team)
- tissues (assurance you will stand behind your children)
- keys (to unlock conversation tools)
- an emergency contact card (of adult role models)

In this chapter, we'll explore the first three of these vital backpack supplies and cover the remaining ones in depth in the chapters that follow. As you read about each item, ask yourself why it's essential and how it could beautifully support your child. Reflect on what you're already doing to equip your child in this area, and be encouraged to stay the course. Also consider which supply is missing or lacking and how you can bridge the gap. The goal is to fill your children's backpacks of faith with essential supplies that will support them, and make sure their packs are strapped on tight before they leave home—not just for elementary school, but for life.

Now let's get started on that supply list. You can do this!

A Water Bottle (Living Water from God's Word)

In Scripture, Jesus first revealed Himself as the awaited Messiah to the Samaritan woman at the well and called Himself "living water." Jesus said to the woman, "If you knew the gift of God and who it is that asks you for a drink, you would have asked him and he would have given you living water. . . . Everyone who drinks this [physical] water will be thirsty again, but whoever drinks the water I give them will never thirst. Indeed, the water I give them will become in them a spring of water welling up to eternal life" (John 4:10, 13-14, NIV).

A water bottle holds water, which is essential to our existence. The good news of Jesus is also essential to our existence. We want our kids to take their spiritual water bottles to school filled to the brim with Jesus. They will get thirsty. What will they turn to when they do? Because harmful cultural elements are rooted in untruth, we must anchor our kids with the truth found in the Word of God and a vibrant relationship with Jesus, our living water. We fill their bottle at home by reading the Bible with them, praying, discussing God's wisdom and their walk with Jesus, and determining life application together. We should also find a faith community for our families that will enrich their lives with Bible-focused teaching for kids their age. If possible, we need to surround them with other trusted adult mentors who will point them to God's truth.

We also provide spiritual hydration by signing our kids up for before- and after-school Bible clubs, Bible-literacy classes, or released-time Bible programs. Your child can never have enough living water!

Many of our most respected leaders have demonstrated that the Bible is the living Word that leads us to Jesus, the source of eternal life. President Abraham Lincoln declared, "[The Bible] is the best gift God has given to man. All the good the Saviour gave to the world was communicated through this book. But for it we could not know right from wrong."[9]

Whether the topic is evolution, gender issues, or the value and meaning of life itself, we must discuss with our kids what God says in His Word about these issues and expose the corresponding untruth or lie. We need to talk about them as often as possible *before* our children encounter them. Then they'll be able to recognize the untruth and respond effectively. Along with prayer (the next step), filling our kids' bottles with the living water of God's Word is the most loving and protective thing we can do as parents. Fear not! When our children encounter something that feels "off," it's the Holy Spirit's job to remind them of what God says about it. They are never truly alone.

A Notebook (God-Confidence Through Prayer)

Not long ago, a funny video went viral on the internet of an adorable preschool girl named Jessica giving herself a pep talk in front of the bathroom mirror. As she stood confidently on the counter, she straddled the sink and enthusiastically sang to her reflection. Her blonde ringlets bounced along as she danced and sang, "I can do anything good! . . . I like my hair! I like my haircuts! . . . I like my room! I like my whole house! . . . Yeah, I can do anything good—better than anyone!"[10]

While healthy self-esteem is good, having confidence only in ourselves, as Jessica clearly did, is not what we want for our kids. Looking to God as the basis for our confidence is best.

Being self-confident sounds admirable, even attainable. The world praises self-made people. "Find your inner strength! You can do it!" it cheers. But loving our kids means steering them toward truth. And here's the truth: They can't navigate life on their own. And God never intended us to! No human has the wisdom, skill, maturity, or capacity to perfectly handle every situation they will encounter in a given day—only God can. Relying solely on ourselves to manage all the demands and expectations of life is quite a heavy burden.

According to a 2021 report from the Barna Group, feelings of failure run rampant in children today. In the Gen Z group surveyed (ages thirteen to twenty-one), 56 percent of young people felt "pressure to be successful," and 42 percent felt "a need to be perfect."[11] With perfection and success as their goal, it's no wonder many Gen Zers are facing an unprecedented mental-health crisis.

So what can we do to combat this?

We, as parents, have the opportunity to breathe truth into our children and relieve this heavy burden before the day even starts. Kids don't have to be self-sufficient or perfect. Reminding our children that God made them and loves them and is with them all day guides them toward the peace that only He can give. Instead of merely giving themselves pep talks like Jessica, our children can have confidence in God's wisdom, skill, and capacity to handle anything life may throw at them. After all, according to the Bible, He created the universe, crafted every cell in their bodies, and numbered every hair on their heads. Our kids are never alone in the challenges they face at school, whether those challenges are academic, physical, social, emotional, or spiritual.

But how do you help your children shift their focus from striving for empty self-confidence to surrendering to the peace of God-confidence, especially on a busy morning when you're trying to get everyone out the door?

Prayer is the answer. Prayer helps our children be God-confident, not self-confident.

As parents, we must teach our kids how to pray. If it seems like prayer should come naturally, remember that the disciples asked Jesus to teach them how to pray (Luke 11:1-4). These Jewish men, whose lives revolved around daily prayers, wanted the intimacy that Jesus so clearly had with His Father. Just as Jesus did with

His disciples, parents have the opportunity to teach and model a dynamic prayer life for their kids. But it's difficult to teach our kids how to depend on God and turn to Him throughout the day for wisdom, discernment, and anything else we need, if we never do it ourselves. We can't model something we aren't actually practicing in our own lives.

So do you turn to God with your needs and the struggles you're facing?

Do you tend to fret about your day instead of seeking God's peace through prayer?

Do you organize and strategize and try to muscle your way through the day alone, or do you put your confidence in God and rely on Him?

I need Jesus to show up in my day. Every day. I need Him to remind me that I am loved and I'm not facing the day alone. I need to take the time to bring my concerns to God and expect Him to show up for me. There are many ways you model this for your children, but let me share with you the prayer habit I established in our home.

I would begin our day with three simple questions. Words matter! They actually set the tone for the entire school day. So I used questions I knew packed a punch. I invite you to borrow my prayer routine until you develop one that works for you. Consider asking your children these three questions every morning:

1. *"Do you know that I love you and the way God made you so [name a quality you see in your child]?"* This affirms to our children that we love them and that God has made them special. Proverbs 16:24 says, "Gracious words are like a

honeycomb, sweetness to the soul and health to the body." Our kids need our affirmations of love.

2. *"What's one thing you're concerned or excited about today?"* This gives kids a safe place to think and talk about what's on their minds. They might be concerned about a school test, a relationship issue, or a sports tryout, or excited about a pizza party or even a snowstorm. When we ask pointed questions and then truly listen without interrupting, our kids feel heard, valued, and connected. Jesus was a master at listening to people, valuing them, and connecting with them.
3. *"Are you ready to pray over your day?"* Take a few moments at breakfast, before you walk out the door in the morning, to pray over the things you just discussed. This will help your children have God-confidence for their day and model what it looks like to take their needs and struggles to Jesus. He has the answers they need. Praying together every morning can become a habit your children love, embrace, and remember to do throughout the day.

Building God-confidence in our children's lives through prayer is undoubtedly one of the most important contributions we can make as parents. British missionary Hudson Taylor wrote, "When we work, we work; but when we pray, God works."[12] The infinite power and protection our children need lie solely in God's hands. Only He can perfectly protect and guide them. And only He can bring about the revival and spiritual awakening we long for in our day.

Rather than worrying about the bad influences our children will encounter during the school day, what if we prayed passionately that God would bring good role models into their lives who will speak truth? We can ask God to move in ways that are undeniably Him. We can ask for wisdom, protection, and the experienced presence of the Lord to be with them. Most importantly, we can pray that God will instill in our children a deep and abiding confidence in Him and talk to Him throughout their school day.

When we pray, God works. Prayer is not passive; it's essential.

Jesus prayed with confidence to His Father in heaven throughout the day and even during the night (Luke 6:12), and we need to teach our children to do the same. Prayer is simply talking to God, praising Him for all He has done in our lives, bringing our requests to Him, and asking Him to provide what we need. Prayer is also about confessing our sins to Him and asking for forgiveness. It's also about bringing all our cares and concerns to Him and laying them at His feet. Psalm 68:19 says, "Praise be to the Lord, to God our Savior, who daily bears our burdens" (NIV).

When we pray, we acknowledge that He is God and we are not. He is a God of detail, and no detail in our lives is too small for His care or too big for Him to handle.

So drink that coffee early every morning and be intentional about your choice of words for your children. Assure them that they are loved, heard, and valued by you and God and that He is with them. Pray with them and for them. Remind them that they can pray anytime, anywhere, and God will hear them. With God-confidence through prayer, they will be fully equipped to face their day.

A Pencil Case (a Safe Place for Questions)

A volunteer small-group leader in one of our Bible2School programs was taken by surprise during a talk about heaven when a little boy at her table asked, "Do you get extra credit if you die at church?"

That's hilarious. But not all the questions our kids ask will be funny. They need to know they have a safe place to ask spiritual questions, and you are that safe place.

Even the sharpest pencils need a pencil case to keep them safe. It's important that your children know that you are a safe place where they can share and ask questions. They need to process any teaching or peer discussion that involves conflicting worldviews. While it's critical to educate our kids on spiritual topics, we must create open communication and intentional space where they can ask or tell us anything. It may be discussing the tension they feel being in the spiritual minority, the confusion of being taught an opposing worldview, or even the difficulty of just being different. Parents must provide a safe place for kids to land with their questions.

Go ahead and practice your "I'm not surprised face," because responding with anger, even righteous anger, or fear isn't going to help prepare them for the road ahead. And it just might shut down communication in the future. Instead, learn to ask good questions, be a safe place for your kids to share, and seek God's wisdom together.

The book of James says, "The testing of your faith produces perseverance. Let perseverance finish its work so that you may be mature and complete, not lacking anything" (1:3-4, NIV). So don't be overly concerned about your child bumping into different worldviews and asking questions. With you as their official safe place—like a pencil case for a sharp pencil—you can help them process things and point them to God's Word to guide them.

Most of us love the season when school supplies begin filling the store aisles. It's a joy to watch our kids' individual personalities shine as they carefully choose the decorative notebooks and folders they like. With this same delight, let's turn to the Lord for help personalizing a plan for equipping our children. What does each child need, and how could you fortify their connection with the Lord? The first three essential backpack supplies—a water bottle brimming with the living water of God's Word, a notebook with heartfelt prayers infusing reliance on God, a pencil case representing a safe place to ask spiritual questions—are all ways we support and nurture our children at home to prepare them for what they'll face at school. Just as we take time to label school supplies with our kids' names, let's take time to ponder their unique styles as we select items to fill their faith backpacks.

Make no mistake. School isn't easy. Conflicts will arise, but the backpack supplies in the next four chapters will equip you and your children to tackle them with wisdom and grace. So dig out your highlighter and get ready for some important coaching. You don't want to miss these tips!

Taking Notes

A little girl came to a Bible2School program one day with a notebook in hand. She wrote feverishly during the large-group lesson and small-group time. When her leader asked why she was writing, the little girl said, "I wanted to take notes because my dad wants to know how to trust in God!"

CHAPTER 11

PLAYING ON THE SAME TEAM

At the beginning of home football games, cheerleaders would stand at the gate and hand out small noisemakers to fans who came to watch our local high school boys play. It wasn't unusual to find me wearing a sweatshirt sporting our team mascot and my son's number as we took our place in the stands. I've seen high school boys play better, find extra motivation, and perhaps even strength, as the home crowd goes wild in encouragement during glorious and difficult moments. The noisemakers, like my cowbell, added to the fun atmosphere, reminding us all of the importance of encouragement.

Surely you've been in the stands when a player's parent becomes hostile rather than helpful. While there are funny reels and memes about "that parent," the truth is, there are always people ready to spew anger, spout negativity, and sow division at the first thing that doesn't go their way. They may yell at the coach about the plays being called, slander other players from the stands, or chew out a ref for a bad call. In actuality, none of this helps. It rarely changes the situation for the better, and quite often it leads to more frustration, causing everyone from players to coaches and refs to react emotionally rather than wisely.

That's why we need to remind ourselves and our children that we are all on the same team. Everyone is deeply invested in our children's well-being and development. As a parent, you are deeply invested in your children, who are doing the hard work of learning to integrate education and faith, as well as their relational and physical development. The outcome of this process is of great importance to you. Teachers have dedicated their lives to educating and mentoring young people.

None of us will be right all the time; that's impossible. But when we function together in unity, we form a dynamic team for the good of our children. Teams function best when they're built on a foundation of trust.

Imagine with me a dynamic and healthy parent-child-teacher relationship. Communication would flow freely and be reciprocal. Parents would be proactively involved in the education of their children, and children would be invested in learning. Teachers would respect the rights of parents and children and honor each family's values. Parents and children would support and respect the investment the teachers make. That's what a solid team approach could look like. Building this kind of team requires unity, and the investment is worth it. We all need to stick together.

If we desire a voice at the table as parents when key decisions are being made for our children, we must begin building a "sticky" relationship of trust today. How can we do that? I'm so glad you asked! Grab a glue stick—the fourth essential item on our supply list—and let's pack it in your child's backpack.

A Glue Stick (to Stick Together as a Team)

Building the educational team we long for can begin as early as day one of the school year. Making the effort to be involved in our children's classes and build relationships with their teachers takes intentionality fueled with precious time and effort. I know none of us think we have time in our day, but we need to make time.

When we intentionally invest in building relationships with our children's teachers, school staff, and even administrators, this effort stands out and increases the likelihood of a better learning environment for our kids. Teachers and staff are often contacted only when problems arise, so encouragement and presence go a long way in developing trust. Start early in the year by getting to know those who are serving and caring for your child during the school day. The investment will yield rich dividends. In fact, the quality of a parent-teacher relationship can make or break your ability to navigate the minefield of religious-rights conversations. Here are a few practical steps you can take:

Introduce yourself. You'd be surprised how many parents don't show up for the school open house or parent-teacher conferences. Taking the time to personally meet your child's teacher is a great first step. Greet the teacher warmly and introduce yourself.

Commit verbally to working together as a team. Take time to let the teacher know that you are a partner in your child's education. This is a great time to express your excitement about the year ahead and your commitment to supporting the teacher's efforts at home. Approaching this partnership intentionally with a servant's heart earns respect. To borrow a famous adage attributed to Teddy

Roosevelt, "People don't care how much you know until they know how much you care."

Look for ways to serve. There is usually no end to the ways you can serve and support public-school teachers. From serving as a homeroom parent, to helping out with party planning or fund-raising, to reading with students, to acting as PTA president, the options are plentiful. Serving begins with a mindset adjustment. You can become a credible ally in the eyes of your child's teacher by esteeming the role of your public-school teachers. Yes, they're paid public servants teaching our children, but have you also considered how deeply they impact the next generation? Here are some questions to routinely ask yourself:

- *How can I humbly serve my children's teachers so they can be excellent at their job, for the sake of my kids and their peers?*
- *How can I support our school staff?*
- *Do my children's teachers need classroom supplies?*
- *Do they need volunteers?*
- *Should I volunteer for a PTA (or other) committee?*
- *What are some ways I can encourage my children's teachers?*

You can stay engaged and connected with your children's teachers throughout the school year by setting a calendar reminder to check in with them periodically. You don't have to spend a lot on a Christmas present to say you care. A simple note thanking them for their kindness and excellence, a homemade treat, or even a note commending them to their principal can be game changing. I've even let my kids' teachers know that we're praying for them! When you make the effort to stay connected throughout the school year, it strengthens the relationship and cultivates trust.

"Should I Attend School Board Meetings?"

The answer is yes. It's our responsibility as parents to be in the know when it comes to our children's education. School boards play a pivotal role in shaping the education that public-school students receive, and they are accountable to the residents in the district that elected them. That's you! The meetings are rich with information on funding sources, curriculum being introduced, mental-health and counseling services being offered to students, the needs of students and their families in the district, new teachers and staff hires, positions that need to be filled, on-campus activities, and clubs being offered to students.

With so much going on, it would be beneficial for your family to attend these meetings.

For more information on this topic, visit bible2school.com and find the blog post titled "3 Benefits of Attending School Board Meetings and How to Take Next Steps."

Give positive, balanced feedback from the beginning. Entering into a healthy partnering relationship with educators is a great way to build trust. And trust is what you need to earn credibility for giving and receiving constructive, helpful feedback. Feedback is critical when religious-rights questions arise. While most think of feedback as criticism, it can be both positive and helpful. Communication in any relationship involves honest and balanced engagement from both parties. Naturally, teachers have a built-in system to give you and your child feedback through homework, test grades, and report cards. But when is it appropriate for *you* to give healthy feedback to a teacher to build trust? Especially if there is conflicting information regarding your child living out their faith in school.

To begin, we must view the healthy giving and receiving of

information and insight about our children and the classroom environment as a positive thing. When we receive a teacher's insights as a gift rather than a threat or criticism of our parenting, both parties win. We also lead the way in opening the door of communication when we *ask* for input from teachers about how our children are doing. While we have history with our kids, teachers have a different vantage point that we need if we want to nurture our children and help them grow. Listening closely during parent-teacher conferences is really important. When we show that we care, we embrace a team approach.

However, parents typically give feedback in the form of a complaint, and that's the only time a teacher will hear from them. I often think that if I were a teacher and had twenty-five sets of parents giving me negative feedback throughout the school year, I'd want to put on my son's football helmet and pads every morning before school to protect my heart. Complaints and negative input don't encourage teachers to do their best. Let's not let this kind of feedback characterize our interactions with teachers and school administrators. We can be different and practice balanced feedback.

Constructive criticism is important, but leading with genuine positive feedback—which I call "essential encouragement"—is, well, essential for productive conversations. Catch teachers doing something good and share that with them first, if possible. This is the most underused feedback tool parents have in their tool belts. Genuine encouragement brings out the best in teachers, freeing them to create a learning environment that brings out the best in our children. Isn't that what we all want?

I've seen the power of a simple note of encouragement. One year I watched my children's dedicated school superintendent get roasted publicly. The media and community were overwhelmingly negative toward her for making an unpopular decision, even though her decision aligned with school policy. She and the school board were under fire for several weeks, but they stood their ground. I happily sent our superintendent a heartfelt email to thank her for doing her job well under fire. I was impressed and grateful for her leadership. She promptly thanked me for my email and shared that she not only appreciated that encouragement, but *she needed it.*

Later that year, an issue arose on my child's sports team that the school athletic director failed to resolve in a timely manner. When I approached the superintendent for help resolving the issue, she was very open to making time for me and listening to my feedback. I'm so grateful I took the time to build a relationship with her before this happened. Our superintendent already knew I valued her. We also had a track record of trust and positive, balanced feedback that made working together to find a solution much easier.

Engaging in the habit of giving positive, balanced feedback—essential encouragement and constructive criticism—shows you value educators. In most cases, they will, in turn, value and respect you as an active, involved parent who cares. Offering positive feedback gives you credibility and a solid foundation for cultivating a partnering relationship with your children's teachers before any conflicts arise.

CONFLICT ISN'T THE PROBLEM

The first month of newlywed blissfulness was coming to an end. My husband, Blaine, waltzed home after work, unaware of what awaited him. As a new bride, I was frustrated. And when I'm upset or frustrated, I usually start cleaning. Our bathroom was sparkling by the time my new husband came home two hours late. Dinner was cold.

When he walked through the doorway, I was ready for a fight. After all, there was no courtesy phone call to inform me of his delay. How could he be so inconsiderate? Like a good wife, I was worried about him. So I angrily rapid-fired questions before he could even put his keys on the counter.

"Where were you? Why didn't you call me? Don't you care about me?"

Blaine was trying to come up for air when I realized by the look on his face that he genuinely had no idea why I was upset. Once he got his bearings, he calmly shared his perspective of the situation. Apparently, he always went out for pizza with his buddies on this day of the month before he was married. He was just following the routine. Of course he cared about me. What was the problem?

The problem was that neither of us had all the facts. We both made assumptions. Neither of us intended any malice. But a breakdown in communication had occurred, and we were at a standstill. In the early years of our marriage, we were afraid of conflict. Now, after over thirty years of marriage, Blaine and I have learned to work through minor (and sometimes major) conflicts and come out better and more productive on the other side. We know we're on the same team. We are going to stick together through thick and thin.

Blaine and I don't always work through conflict perfectly. Still, when we seek to understand each other's perspectives and respectfully listen, we experience incredible benefits in our marriage, home, and parenting.

The same is true of the relationships we all hope to build with those in our public-school systems. Disagreements will arise over the course of our children's school careers. We need to be confident that conflict can be helpful and is sometimes necessary. It doesn't have to lead to strife, especially when all the parties involved are committed to unity. After all, we're on the same team!

ENGAGE: A CASE STUDY ON PARENTAL RIGHTS

I was recently talking with a friend (I'll call her Alicia) who is a typical busy mom on the reserved side. She confessed, "I don't like conflict of any kind, especially when it comes to my child's teacher or school." Then she passionately declared, "But sometimes you have to be strong and have the courage to embrace conflict, like Joshua in the Bible, because it's our job [as parents] to make sure our children have a safe environment at home *and* at school."

Alicia had recently practiced courage in a rising conflict. Her son had brought home a required-reading book from his teacher, Mrs. C., that was not only inappropriate for his age but was also inappropriate in general: It glorified and encouraged involvement in teen sex, drugs, and alcohol. Her son brought the book to his mother because he felt uncomfortable. Alicia read it from cover to cover and was concerned.

Why would a public school require kids to read that kind of content?

Alicia was shocked, angered, and saddened all at the same time. How could she protect her son's mind from this type of message when it was required school reading? What was the best course of action to protect her child and yet maintain a good relationship with Mrs. C. and the school?

Most parents would rather have a tooth extracted than step into a difficult discussion with their child's teacher. Alicia decided to start with prayer.

Pave the Way with Prayer

Our God promises wisdom when we ask for it, and when difficult situations like these arise, we certainly need wisdom. Part of receiving God's wisdom is evaluating the facts and then humbly evaluating ourselves. Alicia began praying and asking for wisdom. She also called friends to pray with her.

In Matthew 18:19, Jesus said, "I tell you that if two of you on earth agree about anything they ask for, it will be done for them by my Father in heaven" (NIV). Alicia knew she needed prayer support, so she asked her small group to pray for three crucial things for her and her son's teacher: God's wisdom, soft hearts, and effective communication for a God-pleasing outcome.

Evaluate the Facts, Evaluate Yourself

I was so proud of my friend Alicia because she took time to prayerfully evaluate the situation. It takes humility to double-check the facts. It's so easy to "shoot, ready, aim" when it comes to conflict. Alicia did the work to make sure she understood the assignment and the book in question. Then she checked the book's message against the Bible, the cornerstone of their family's faith. Finally, she sought wise Christian counsel and asked herself these questions:

1. *Does this book's message align with our family's faith values?*
2. *Am I overreacting?*

3. *What is the real issue?*
4. *Is there a legal component?*
5. *Do I feel strongly enough about this to act?*

The answers clarified the situation:

1. No, this book did *not* align with the Bible or her family's faith values.
2. No, she was not overreacting, since this type of messaging could harm her son's mind or any other child's mind.
3. Clearly, the real issues were the fact that the school was subjecting her son to harmful content and violating her family's religious beliefs and values.
4. Yes, there was a legal parental-rights issue.
5. Yes, she did feel strongly enough about this issue to act.

Fortunately, Alicia understood her right as a parent to question the curriculum choices of her school. She and her husband knew that a book that glamorizes alcohol, substance abuse, and teen sex would likely raise flags for other parents as well. They decided to get in the game and advocate for their son.

WHAT ARE PARENTAL RIGHTS?

According to Alliance Defending Freedom,

> Parents, not the government, have the right to raise their children. . . . Parental rights include, but are not limited to, making decisions regarding children's education and health care in a manner consistent with their family's

> beliefs. . . . Every parent has not only the right but the duty to care for their children. . . . [These rights] are fundamental and universal, and they cannot be given or taken away by any government.[1]

Not having a safe environment for all families' faith values can directly affect a child's upbringing and, therefore, conflict with parental rights. Alicia and her husband agreed that their son and other children's minds were at stake because the public school was requiring them to read inappropriate information that was, in their eyes, harmful to their son's growth and development. They concluded that Alicia needed to meet with Mrs. C. and discuss the assignment.

Showing Value Through Preparation

Making sure you have all the correct information *before* you contact a teacher shows that you value their time. My husband once had a naval commander who always said, "Trust but verify." Alicia didn't just rely on her son as the sole source of information about the reading assignment. If you skip the fact-checking aspect of preparing for a discussion with your child's teacher, you might end up having unnecessary conversations and confrontations.

Take a moment to outline your concerns and questions. Bullet-point the major issues. Then ask yourself, *What do I want the outcome to be?* Being thoughtful with your words shows you value the teacher as a person.

Also ask yourself, *What are the implications for my child in this situation, and how might other children be impacted?* Asking this question demonstrates that you value your child and all the children involved in the situation.

Taking time to prepare for a sensitive discussion with a teacher will help bring unity and clarity to the conversation.

Schedule a Meeting

Start by scheduling a meeting directly with your child's teacher. Many parents ask, "Should you communicate with your child's teacher in person or through email?" The answer is both. Start with an email or written form of communication requesting a meeting and share the general topic you would like to discuss. This allows the teacher to prepare for the discussion and gives you time to think through your words and your tone before the interaction. Tone is everything. Yours should be one of curiosity and respect. You're trying to understand the requirement and the underlying reason as it relates to your child's overall learning experience. Your communication also needs to convey respect for the teacher's time and availability. (See the appendix for a resource on this.)

It takes courage to stand up when a conflict arises with a teacher or school administrators, but remember that you are modeling the very courage your children will need to walk out their faith in a secular world. Remember, the goal is working through conflict with unity to develop trust that sticks. When you've done the work to build trust with school administrators and teachers, they'll be less likely to become defensive when you raise concerns. You'll also earn credibility with them through encouragement, and your child will benefit.

In the next chapter, we'll discuss how to handle conflicts when your child's religious rights have been violated. Don't worry, we'll hear the rest of Alicia's story as we walk through the steps to kindly educate the educators.

The Walking Bible

A third grader shared with his mom that he is now known as the "Walking Bible" in his class. When his friends told him they believe in the big-bang idea, he went to his desk and got out the Bible he kept there. Then he confidently opened it up to Genesis and showed them that God made the earth and everything in it.

CHAPTER 12

KINDLY EDUCATING THE EDUCATORS

Alicia wiped her sweaty palms on her dress pants as her heels clicked loudly down the school corridor. She was on her way to talk to her son's teacher, Mrs. C., in person, and quick prayers fluttered through her mind. Conflict wasn't easy, but she knew the Holy Spirit was prompting her to have this discussion. Alicia had met all her son's teachers, and Mrs. C. was especially kind. She knew this conversation might be uncomfortable, but she was grateful they'd already built some trust.

As Alicia approached the classroom, Mrs. C. opened her door with a tentative smile and welcomed her into the empty room. After a few minutes of exchanging pleasantries with Mrs. C., Alicia started the conversation.

ALICIA: Thank you for all you do for our students. Our son really enjoys your class. However, as I said in my email, my husband and I have some concerns about the content of our son's required-reading assignment. My son brought the book to me and expressed concern about the content. After reading it, I, too, was concerned because it has many references to sex, drugs, and getting drunk. It seems to encourage this behavior, and that doesn't align with our family values. I know we both want the best for my child, but I was wondering what your thoughts were behind this required book assignment? Can you please help me understand why you chose this book?

MRS. C.: I understand. When I first ordered it, I, too, was shocked. The middle school teaching magazines highly recommend it. It's just one book on the required-reading list, but I don't want your son or any of my students to be uncomfortable. I'll help him pick another book for this assignment. And I'll seriously consider putting this book on the parent-permission-only list. Thanks for making me aware of your concerns.

ALICIA: Thank you for understanding and being willing to help our son. It's surprising that this book is highly recommended. We're concerned about the impact this book may have on the other students as well. It would ease our minds if we knew that other parents also had a chance to review this book before their children read it.

MRS. C.: As a mother myself, I completely understand and agree. In fact, I've toyed with that idea myself. Parents really should be given the opportunity to review what their children are required to read. After hearing your concerns, I'm definitely adding this book to the permission-only list for next semester. Thanks again for helping me make that decision.

Wow. Was it the trust Alicia had so obviously cultivated before this conversation that made a difference? Was it the prayers she had prayed for hearts to be prepared and open, or her thorough preparation? Honestly, it all mattered in that moment, and God moved on her behalf. I'm so proud of my friend and the steps she took to "kindly educate" her son's teacher and advocate for him and his peers. What a gift to have a team approach with your educator!

Truthfully, not all conflicts resolve as easily as this one did, but the best approach to conflict resolution is the same. Unknowingly, Alicia used the steps I now call the ABCs of Kindly Educating.

THE ABCS OF KINDLY EDUCATING

As I shared, I'm a mom and the leader of a nonprofit ministry serving public-school families. I also have more than twenty-five years of experience interacting with teachers, principals, and superintendents. Many times over the years, seemingly opposite viewpoints were brought to the table, but everyone would agree on the main goal: *the healthy growth and development of our children.* These experiences helped me develop the ABCs of Kindly Educating, an effective six-step communication approach for navigating conflict situations:

Assume the best.
Be curious.
Clarify your concern.
Defend the truth confidently.
Engage in collaboration.
Follow up fantastically.

Assume the Best

Assuming the best about others is not our natural go-to when entering uncharted territory. We're protective and skeptical beings, especially when it comes to our kids. But when we slow down to pray and humbly evaluate our thoughts, it helps us remember to assume the best about others, not the worst. That includes educators. The kindest thing you can do for your children's teachers when it comes to conflict is to assume the best about their intentions and motivations. Alicia took time to ponder the fact that God loves Mrs. C. She isn't the enemy. In this "us versus them" world, it's easy to slip into this toxic mindset when it comes to our kids' teachers. Alicia assumed the best about Mrs. C., and her countenance affirmed it. Alicia's nonverbal communication before she even walked in the room was the opposite of attacking—it was kind.

Be Curious

Because Alicia desired to understand the reasoning behind Mrs. C.'s book choice for the required-reading assignment, she took a posture of curiosity. She asked questions and she listened. Alicia started the conversation by expressing appreciation for Mrs. C. and then asked a question: "I know we both want the best for my child, but I was wondering what your thoughts were behind this required book assignment?" Then she followed up with a request: "Can you please help me understand why you chose this book?"

If clarity isn't achieved in the conversation after starting off with honoring language and curious questions, follow-up questions are appropriate. A question like "Can you tell me more about that?" helps others articulate their reasoning so that you can determine whether conflict truly exists.

When kindly educating others, the skill of listening well is key.

John Wooden, a famous Christian basketball coach, wisely said, "Listen if you want to be heard."[1] This proved to be true in Alicia's conversation.

Clarify Your Concern

Most educators want the best for our children, but we need to realize they can get it wrong sometimes. Your child's teacher might be following educational guidelines or a school policy you don't know about. Teachers can be misinformed and not realize their actions are interfering with your parental rights or your child's religious rights.

To introduce her concerns about the book, Alicia let Mrs. C. know that she had read it and found "many references to sex, drugs, and getting drunk." Then she clarified her concerns by explaining to Mrs. C. that the book "doesn't align with our family values."

Mrs. C. admitted to Alicia that she was "shocked" when she first ordered the book, because it had been highly recommended.

At this point, Alicia could have sought further clarification on what she thought she heard the teacher say: "So what I'm hearing you say is that you also had some concerns about the appropriateness of this book, even though it was highly recommended. Is that right?"

Clarification is key so the teacher can correct any misconceptions you might have. It also reveals what the teacher is basing their decisions or actions on and why. This often saves the time and energy of challenging something that might not even be an issue.

After Mrs. C. thanked Alicia for sharing her concerns about the book's potential impact on her son, Alicia provided additional clarification by expressing her concerns about its impact on other students as well. Mrs. C. wholeheartedly agreed with Alicia, affirming her own concerns about the book and helping her reach a decision about placing the book on a permission-only list that would require parents to review the content before allowing their children to read it.

In Alicia's case, clarifying her concerns led to a positive outcome.

Defend the Truth Confidently

Because Alicia consistently nurtured trust in her relationship with Mrs. C., prepared well for their conversation, and communicated her concerns in a kind and respectful way, she was able to confidently defend the truth and the family values she held dear. And Mrs. C. was open to hearing her concerns.

Like Alicia, all American parents have the freedom to exercise their parental rights and responsibility to direct the upbringing of their children, including the right to question school assignments. When school curriculum doesn't align with our family values, we have the right to speak up, request a change or accommodation, and ultimately remove our children from a situation if necessary.

Sometimes we, as parents, need to help educators stay in their legal lane when it comes to religious rights as well. One mom shared with me that when she tried to legally start a released-time Bible program at her public elementary school, the principal repeatedly declined to meet with her. But this persistent mom finally met with both the principal and the superintendent and kindly educated them. She confidently defended the truth about exercising religious rights for public-school students.

As we discussed earlier, released-time Bible programs are legal if they are held off campus, no tax funds are used, and parents have permitted their children to attend. This reluctant principal was actually fearful of letting students participate in an off-campus "religious program" because "other religions would want to have programs too." But the truth is that this principal was impeding all children's religious rights protected under the Constitution. By not allowing this mother to start a Bible program, this educator's actions were, in fact, not upholding the law. So this mom followed the ABCs of Kindly Educating the educators and helped the school stay in its legal lane.

Engage in Collaboration

Even if it takes more than one meeting, like the Bible-program mom's situation did, your child is worth the effort. A willingness to collaborate with our children's teachers demonstrates that we want to be part of the solution to the conflict.

My friend Alicia came to the conversation table prepared to collaborate with Mrs. C. and brainstorm creative solutions. She had even prayed over possible solutions to share with her son's teacher. But as it turned out, after Alicia shared her concerns, Mrs. C. thoughtfully responded with one of the solutions Alicia had thought of: letting her son choose another book that would satisfy the required-reading assignment and honor her family values. But Mrs. C. went even further: She decided to put the book on the parent-permission only list so it wouldn't be required reading. Problem solved. Alicia was so grateful. The relationship between parent and teacher was preserved and deepened through kindly educating Mrs. C., and the responsibility for her son's education was back in Alicia's hands.

Follow Up Fantastically

I have a rule of thumb when it comes to meeting with anyone: Always, always, always follow up fantastically with written communication. That means sending an email that recaps the problem discussed, the solution agreed upon, the action steps assigned, and the timeline to get them done. After meeting with Mrs. C., Alicia made sure she sent her a clear, kind email that followed up fantastically. This dispelled the likelihood of future conflicts caused by fuzzy memories of what happened at the meeting and a lack of clarity on solutions and next steps.

Another element of following up fantastically after kindly educating your child's teacher is letting them know when you have completed your assigned action steps. This is a common courtesy, and it encourages the teacher to keep you informed about the status of their action steps as well. And it reinforces your mutual efforts to stick together as a team.

Although it seems old-fashioned, when you take the time to write a handwritten note to your child's teacher, thanking them for their willingness to listen and collaborate on a solution that ensures a safe environment for your child's faith to flourish, it will bless them tremendously. In our hurry-up world, slowing down and going the extra mile shows how much you appreciate and value the teacher as a partner in your child's educational journey. It's a nice touch that nurtures the parent-teacher relationship, which we know is vital. (See the appendix for a resource with the ABCs of talking points.)

Preserving Your Testimony

A word of caution while you're waiting for the resolution of an issue: Stay the course and keep doing the right thing. Strengthen your faith testimony by refusing to angrily attack others, slander the teacher or school administrators publicly on social media, or malign their character through gossip. It will be a temptation, but God will help you through this journey. Stay grounded in prayer. There is no need to defame someone else in this process. By resisting temptation, you preserve your testimony with your child, your family, your school, and your community.

NICOLE'S STORY: A SUPPRESSION OF RELIGIOUS RIGHTS

Nicole was a sweet eight-year-old, excitedly looking forward to her upcoming class Halloween party. She was thrilled about picking just the right treat to hand out to all her classmates. Who doesn't get excited about handing out candy to their friends and playing party games? But Nicole had something extra that cranked her excitement up a notch. She had prepared a Bible verse to attach to the candy. Because her family made it a priority to share their faith when appropriate with those around them, Nicole was not only handing out her *favorite candy*; she was also attaching her *favorite Bible verse*, John 3:16: "For God so loved the world, that he gave his only Son, that whoever believes in him should not perish but have eternal life." Nicole's mom respectfully informed the teacher of Nicole's idea the day before the party.

The morning of the party, Nicole and her mom carefully packed her Halloween treats in her backpack in anticipation of the afternoon party. As her mother was cleaning up the breakfast dishes, she got a call from the school superintendent. He let her know that Nicole's treat for the Halloween party was not allowed because it had a Bible verse on it. Nicole could either remove the Bible verse from each piece of candy or not hand out her treats. Nicole was devastated over the news.

After briefly talking it over with her mom, Nicole decided to remove the verse. Tears flowed freely as she quickly tore off the verse she had lovingly attached to each treat. Then she headed out the door to the bus stop. In the quiet after Nicole had left, her mom pondered the situation. *This doesn't sound right,* she thought. *Isn't this a religious-liberty violation? Should I challenge the superintendent's decision?*

When our children feel like their religious liberties are being violated, it's confusing to them. Sometimes tears flow. That's why they need us to stand behind them with discernment. Nicole's desire to share her faith was precious, and her mom was so sad for her as she left the house. Her gut feeling was right. Nicole's religious liberties had been violated. So her mom took the next step. It was time to kindly educate the educators, but before she did, she whispered a prayer for her child.

When situations like this happen, we need to add the fifth essential backpack supply to support our kids.

Tissues (Assurance You Will Stand Behind Your Children)

As parents, we sometimes need to defend and maintain the boundaries of our children's religious freedom so they have continuity in living out their faith at home and at school. As my children's first-string discipler, I know firsthand that advocating is one of the hardest things a parent will do, but our children are worth it.

If your kids are like mine, they're not always right. My boys generated their fair share of notes home from their teachers. When our kids are wrong, it's important to back the teacher. But there are times when teachers are wrong and infringe on our children's religious liberties. That's when we need to investigate the legal facts and see if the school's position aligns with the Constitution and students' rights. We also need to assure our kids that we will stand behind them. This often gives them the confidence they need to courageously defend religious liberties and freely express their faith in public school.

Not all situations will require us to take action, but keep in mind that our rights as parents are protected, and we can speak up if something is amiss. Most of the time, we can simply coach our children on how to handle violations of their religious rights.

But in some cases, we need to be willing to kindly educate those in authority.

Let's get back to Nicole's story. The next day, even though the party was over, Nicole's mom decided to follow the ABCs of Kindly Educating her child's educators. She called me and others, asking us to pray and pave the way for her to challenge this school decision. Nicole's mom had a great relationship with the teacher and assumed the best about her and the other school administrators. *They must be mistaken*, she thought.

She then called a cousin who is a judge, and he told her that the school was not staying in their legal lane with this decision. Yes, the school must stay neutral on religion. However, by forbidding Nicole's religious speech—handing out candy with her favorite Bible verse attached—they were *not* neutral and had violated the First Amendment.

Nicole's mom decided to call the superintendent back and ask some clarifying questions. During the conversation, she stayed respectfully curious and clarified her concern: "It was my understanding that the teacher wasn't handing out the treats. This was a student-to-student transaction, and I thought that was allowed in public school."

The superintendent told her they had checked with their school lawyer (solicitor), and he affirmed that their decision was legal. She thanked him for the clarification and kindly educated him by defending the truth according to the Constitution: In denying her daughter's religious speech, they were *not* remaining neutral. She did her best to present more facts and engage in collaboration to resolve the issue, but to no avail. The superintendent was adamant that the school's position on the matter was legally correct.

WHEN KINDLY EDUCATING DOESN'T WORK

Even if you follow the ABCs of Kindly Educating the educators, they may refuse to rectify the situation and align school policy or their decisions with your parental rights or your child's constitutionally protected religious rights. This was the case for Nicole's mom.

If this happens, your next step is to ask to talk to the school solicitor. This person's job is to keep the school in its legal lane, so make sure to follow the ABCs of Kindly Educating during your conversation. If things don't change after speaking to the school solicitor, it's time to seek legal advice from lawyers who specialize in religious freedom. Two reputable organizations that can help you find these legal services are Alliance Defending Freedom and First Liberty Institute.

In Nicole's case, her mom decided to talk to a lawyer. She followed up fantastically by sending a letter to the superintendent and the president of the school board, letting them know that their decision not to let Nicole hand out Halloween treats with her favorite Bible verse was unconstitutional. Religious speech initiated by a student is protected in the same way nonreligious speech is protected. And it keeps the school neutral on religion.

Why go to this next level? Not only are you protecting your child, but you're also seeking to correct false beliefs and actions that erode constitutional rights, damage communities, and ultimately harm all children in the public-school system for present and future generations. So tap into God's strength and courage, because you're helping make things right for your child, your family, your school, and your community. And you are doing it kindly!

Within days of receiving the letter from Nicole's family attorney, the school reversed its decision about the Halloween candy and the Bible verse. In fact, the solicitor oversaw eight other schools and was able to lift the restrictions at those schools as well. Because her mom got off the bleachers, Nicole could now share treats and a Bible verse at the next class party. She was free to live out her faith in public school as she saw fit—and so were her classmates.

In the next chapter, we'll equip your children with some key tools for sharing their faith and navigating difficult conversations when others challenge their faith.

Teaching My Little Sister

While attending a released-time Bible program, a little girl diligently learned an interactive rhyme with hand motions that traced the chronological events of the Old Testament. She loved it so much, she shared excitedly, "I'm teaching it to my little sister at home!"

CHAPTER 13

CONVERSATION TOOLS FOR KIDS

"Mr. Lane, your dashboard light is blinking. It needs to be fixed. And the chewed gum you stuck over it, so you don't have to see it, doesn't really work. You need to take your van to a repair shop!"

I was a bit embarrassed by my young son's honest but rude response to a friend's question, "How do you like my van?"

Thankfully, my son's lack of conversational etiquette didn't faze our good-natured friend, and he took the comment in stride. The old adage that "kids say the darndest things"[1] was alive and well at our house.

As parents, *we* don't always know what to say in a given situation, especially when it comes to matters of faith. *Is it the right time to say something or not?* Do our kids feel the same awkwardness?

Truthfully, kids sometimes handle faith conversations better than we do. At other times, however, they need our coaching to develop this skill set. Practicing how to handle possible conversation scenarios can help our kids feel more confident about sharing their faith.

As parents, we make mistakes in conversations, and our kids are going to make mistakes too. But we want them to be equipped with conversation tools as they go out into the world, especially when it comes to their faith. We want them to be able to "[speak] the truth in love" (Ephesians 4:15) and have discernment, knowing when to speak and when to stay silent. We want them to honor God and others with their words.

Because public school is a dynamic mixture of children from all sorts of backgrounds, our kids are exposed to a variety of socioeconomic, cultural, moral, and religious influences different from our own. It can be unnerving that, as parents, we can no longer shield them from outside influences. You may wonder, *Will my children be bullied when it becomes apparent they are Christians? Will they be able to handle those difficult conversations?*

As first-string disciplers, we want to make sure our children have the conversation tools they need. Sharing their faith proactively and responding in godly ways when others question their beliefs are skills we don't want our children to be without. That's why we need to slip the sixth essential supply into their backpacks: keys to unlock conversation tools for the challenges they'll encounter.

Keys (to Unlock Conversation Tools)

Keys unlock important things for kids—like their houses or their bike locks. They can also unlock precious tools. When I was growing up, my dad always kept whatever he needed to fix our car in his toolbox in the trunk. Getting to his tools required the car keys. Giving kids keys that unlock precious conversation tools for talking with others about their faith is just as important. With a rise in nonverbal communication, like texting and group chats, our children are presented with fewer opportunities to practice verbal communication skills. Bold statements of faith that spark emotions get a lot of attention, and kids often lack conversation tools for handling these scenarios.

But don't worry! I have your back. In this chapter, we'll unpack the keys that unlock two types of tools your children will need to navigate tricky faith conversations at school: *responding in a godly way* and *sharing faith proactively*. You'll see each of these tools in action in different fictional scenarios to role-play with your child. After each scenario, I'll provide some coaching nuggets for you and your child to discuss.

Begin by reading through each scenario with your child, and then role-play the conversation together. Or you can personalize a real-life scenario your child experienced in the past and brainstorm some fresh ideas together on how your child could have responded in a godly way. To speak confidently, our kids need us to practice with them so they'll understand the heart behind these ideas. Even if the role-playing seems a little awkward, it's important to help them feel prepared. So let's make sure they have the tools they need to unlock conversations about Jesus.

RESPONDING IN A GODLY WAY

The Bible has a lot to say about interacting with others—especially those who don't align with our faith in Christ. First Peter 3:15 says, "In your hearts revere Christ as Lord. Always be prepared to give an answer to everyone who asks you to give the reason for the hope that you have. But do this with gentleness and respect" (NIV). We should expect that other students, and even educators, at public school will ask our kids why they're so different from their peers. As parents, we pray that our children will walk with integrity, even when their peers do not, and that their speech will be marked with sincerity, kindness, and purity. We also pray their behavior will reflect a life of courage, love, and compassion that is grounded in Jesus.

It's important for children to know they're not alone when they live out their faith in a public-school environment. In John 15:18, Jesus said to His followers, "If the world hates you, remember that it hated me first" (NLT). But how do you prepare your kids for this? What can they say when conversations turn hostile to their faith?

Learning how to respond in a godly way can help our kids navigate three faith-challenging scenarios they may face at school: *an untruth presented as truth*, *an attacking statement*, or *a mistaken directive*. Share the following scenarios with your children to illustrate how they can respond with respect when friction occurs.

An Untruth Presented as Truth

Tyler settled into his chair in biology class and flipped open his laptop. As he scanned the list of upcoming assignments, he noticed they would be learning how genetic traits are carried and passed on from one generation to the next. He had heard this happens with eye color, and even color blindness, and he was interested in learning more, since he was color-blind but his parents were not.

Tyler discovered that, according to science, parents pass down the genes for red-green color-vision deficiency through the X chromosome. His mother, with XX chromosomes, had passed on the color-blind gene to him on an X chromosome, but his dad, with XY chromosomes, couldn't have passed on the gene because he contributed Tyler's Y chromosome. Tyler was fascinated to learn that some genetic traits could be carried by a parent and fully affect one child if the right combination of genes was present.

As Tyler was pondering these new revelations, his thoughts were interrupted by a classmate who suggested to the class that chromosomes didn't really matter when it came to being male or female, because you could choose your own gender. Rather than brushing the statement aside and moving on, the teacher invited the class to weigh in on this comment. The ensuing conversation went something like this:

TEACHER: Class, let's open this up for discussion. What are your thoughts on gender, given some of the science we've been exploring?

CLASSMATE: That's easy! Gender is fluid, and you can choose whatever you want to be based on how you feel. Genetics might determine your eye color, but your feelings are yours to control. We see it all the time, like when someone who was assigned female at birth just isn't into all the clothes and makeup and girly stuff. And what about the guys who do want to wear makeup and nail polish? You can't tell me their likes and dislikes are wrong.

TYLER: I'm curious about your point that what a person likes or dislikes is a factor in determining their gender. What if a girl wants to play on the football team, which is typically a male-dominated sport, but she doesn't think she's a male? How would you explain that?

CLASSMATE: Well, it's up to each person to figure that out for themselves. And you're right. A girl could play on the football team, but probably as the kicker. Then she's not playing a position where she's tackling people, because girls would be at a disadvantage trying to tackle a guy.

TYLER: So I hear you saying that girls are different than guys, because one has the potential to be physically stronger. Based on our study of chromosomes, wouldn't you say that the girl can't change her DNA? That the chromosomes she was born with are fixed and can't be altered?

CLASSMATE: Yes, she wouldn't be able to change her DNA. Don't be silly. You get what you get. But if she feels like a guy and wants to be a guy, she should be able to choose that.

TYLER: But her feelings wouldn't change her DNA or physical makeup?

CLASSMATE: Right.

TYLER: If we agree on the facts that DNA can't be altered, and 99 percent of people are definitively born with XX or XY chromosomes, and we call those with XX chromosomes females and those with XY chromosomes males, then how can gender be fluid, if the definition of male and female can't be altered?

CLASSMATE: I don't know. It's just how you feel. Everyone should get to choose.

TYLER: I respectfully disagree with you. In this case, science backs up what the Bible says in Genesis: that God created us male and female. If God is doing the creating, then it's out of our control. There's nothing in the Bible that says males and females can't like different things, but likes or dislikes don't determine a person's gender. God does.

With that closing statement, the bell rang and class was dismissed. Tyler was curious how the rest of his class would react to the discussion they had just heard. He knew some of them weren't believers, and he hoped that what they were learning and discussing would open the door for more conversations about how science provides evidence that God is a remarkable Creator.

Let's note how Tyler handled this conversation in a godly way:

- *He was curious and treated his classmate with respect.* Tyler expressed curiosity by asking questions to help draw out his classmate's reasoning rather than jumping to conclusions. Then he respectfully listened to his classmate's responses and asked clarifying questions. Even when he disagreed, he did so in a respectful way.
- *He stated facts.* Tyler supported his position with facts about chromosomes and DNA that the class had established as being true. He then used those facts to draw his conclusions clearly.
- *He was patient.* Rather than lead with his faith in the conversation, Tyler took some time to establish rapport with his classmate. As a result, the rest of the class could listen and engage as Tyler winsomely restated the scientific facts they were all learning and then tied them to the truth presented in the Bible.

It's not unusual for kids to be called unkind names like "bigot" or "fanatic" when they express their religious views at school. If this happens to your children, and they come to you to talk about it, praise God! Listen with compassion. Affirm them for handling things in a way that honors God. Let them know that God knows and sees everything, and He is with them. Even though it may feel unpleasant at the time, rubbing up against the world actually strengthens their faith. When they suffer for following Christ, Jesus promises a great reward in heaven (Matthew 5:11-12).

An Attacking Statement

Nick had an epic summer. He attended his first-ever live concert by his favorite Christian band. He had saved his money from mowing lawns to buy one of the band's T-shirts after the show, and he wore the shirt everywhere. He had a joy-filled mountaintop experience at the concert, worshiping with hundreds of other Christians. Every time he put on the shirt, he got a little chill as the memories came flooding back.

The shirt was also special because his favorite Bible verse was printed on it. Glancing down at the verse reminded him how much God loved him, and he felt a sense of peace and belonging every time he saw it. Nick was excited to wear his new T-shirt on the first day of school. In fact, he secretly hoped that others would see it and catch some of that feeling of God's joy for themselves.

Nick eagerly greeted his friends on the way to school and told them about his amazing concert experience. Nick felt terrific as they fist-bumped him in approval. When he arrived at school, Nick found his new homeroom and took his assigned seat (arranged in alphabetical order). Sitting across from him was a classmate he didn't know. The teacher asked students to turn to their neighbors and share one highlight from the summer.

As Nick turned to the boy across from him, eager to share his concert experience, his classmate spoke first: "What are you doing wearing a shirt like that? You're not some sort of Holy Roller, are you? I bet you'd rat on me if you saw me cheating on a test."

Nick's balloon of excitement suddenly burst. But instead of reacting defensively, he took a deep breath and offered a kind and genuine reply: "Thanks for commenting on my shirt. It actually represents something that's really important to me, just like I'm sure your shirt represents something that's important to you. I'm really curious to know you better and was going to ask you to tell me more about your shirt. Do you have a favorite memory from Yellowstone?"

Nick's neighbor seemed surprised and looked down at the Yellowstone National Park emblem on his T-shirt. Then he excitedly shared about his family trip to the park that summer, where he saw geysers and buffalo.

When it was Nick's turn to share his concert experience, his classmate listened quietly.

In spite of the unexpected start to the conversation, Nick chose to respond in a godly way:

- *He controlled his emotions.* Nick likely felt disappointment, anger, and possibly even a twinge of fear, but instead of letting his emotions control his response, he took a deep, calming breath to compose himself before responding.
- *He was gracious.* Nick's gracious expression of thanks surprised his neighbor. That simple act of courtesy and kindness

defused a tense situation and neutralized his classmate's reaction.

- *He stated a fact.* In sharing that his concert T-shirt was important to him, Nick stated a fact that his classmate couldn't refuse. Only Nick could determine what was important to him.
- *He was curious.* Nick expressed curiosity about his classmate's Yellowstone T-shirt and invited him to share about his experience. This question showed Nick's willingness to hear what his classmate had to say before sharing his own summer experience.

When our children intentionally live out their faith at school, people can tell they're different from those around them. They don't cut corners on assignments or lie or disrespect teachers or pick on other students. These are the marks of a godly life.

One friend shared that her child apologized to a teacher for something, and the astonished teacher said, "In all my years of teaching, I have never had a student apologize to me."

Of course, our kids aren't perfect, but living differently from the world will give them plenty of opportunities to offer godly responses when others attack their faith. And it will open doors for them to share the hope that shines in their hearts.

A Mistaken Directive

Meg burst into the house, her usual energy heightened by the news she couldn't wait to share with her family. Her class was getting ready for its annual history showcase! Inspired by last year's showcase, where students presented themselves as historical figures, she had in mind a person they had been learning about in church lately: Ruth, the great-grandmother of King David in the Bible. Ruth's example of faith and courage was inspiring to Meg.

The next day, Meg submitted her selection to her teacher and started to pull together her costume and speaking points. When her submission came back with a "Please see me" on the top, Meg thought perhaps her teacher wasn't aware of Ruth and needed some clarification. The conversation, however, wasn't what Meg expected.

TEACHER: So, Meg, I got your submission for the history showcase. That's terrific! With your high-energy personality, I'm sure you'll give a great presentation. There's just the one little issue regarding the person you've chosen to present. This is a person talked about in the Bible. Could you tell me more about her?

MEG: Yes, Ruth is mentioned in the Bible, and there's actually a whole book devoted to her story. She showed great faith and courage in difficult circumstances, and I've really been inspired by her. I'm excited to tell others about her!

TEACHER: Well, as good as that sounds, I'm afraid I'll have to ask you to share about another person. We can't have a biblical figure in the history showcase. Separation of church and state, you know.

MEG: Actually, I don't know. Could you explain?

TEACHER: Well, separation of church and state means that we can't allow anything religious to be talked about or discussed here at school. It might look like the school is favoring a particular religion, and then who knows what would happen. People might get upset, I might lose my job, and the history showcase might be canceled outright. We just can't take the chance of offending someone.

MEG: Okay. I'd like to talk this over with my parents and get their ideas too. Can I talk with you again soon?

TEACHER: Sure, but please be thinking of another historical figure in the meantime. I can't wait to see what you come up with.

Let's highlight the godly ways Meg handled this situation:

- *She was curious.* Meg had heard the phrase *separation of church and state* before but wasn't exactly sure what it meant. Instead of arguing with the teacher or acting out in frustration, she asked a follow-up question. This helped her understand her teacher's reasoning for asking Meg to choose a nonbiblical figure, as well as how her teacher defined *separation of church and state.*
- *She was patient and knew she needed more information.* Something felt off about what her teacher said about the separation of church and state, but Meg didn't quite know what it was. Instead of discussing a topic she wasn't sure about, or simply accepting the teacher's explanation, Meg opted to patiently wait until she knew she had the right information before responding to her teacher's decision.
- *She put the conversation on pause.* Even though her teacher was eager to check this off her list and move on, Meg asked

> for another conversation after talking with her parents and hearing their ideas. In the teacher's mind, the decision had been made, and Meg would have to choose another historical figure. But Meg still had questions. In asking for another conversation, she left the door open for more discussion.

Meg's teacher gave her the wrong information based on a faulty understanding of what separation of church and state means. Meg's parents could have handled the situation themselves, but they decided to coach their daughter on advocating for herself. Meg was glad they were available if she needed their help clarifying facts, proofreading emails, and answering questions. This type of coaching builds our children's confidence for handling crucial faith conversations on their own.

In all these scenarios, Tyler, Nick, and Meg offered godly responses in different faith-challenging scenarios. They not only listened respectfully but also stated the truth in a grace-filled way. They kept their cool, they were curious, and they were patient. Offering a godly response isn't easy in the moment, but with this conversation tool under their belt and with our coaching, our children will be well prepared to navigate even the most challenging interactions.

SHARING FAITH PROACTIVELY

Following His resurrection, Jesus gave His disciples this final command before returning to His Father in heaven: "Go into all the world and preach the gospel to all creation" (Mark 16:15, NIV). The great commission is for our children as well.

Besides knowing how to respond when their faith is challenged, our kids also need to know when it's appropriate to share their faith. The First Amendment protects our right to respond as well as to initiate religious conversations. But as parents, we need to teach our children how to exercise their rights in a way that is respectful, engaging, and welcoming.

When Jesus is part of your conversations at home, it will be natural for your children to include Him in their conversations at school.

Let's explore three scenarios that illustrate how children can share their faith proactively: *distributing religious materials*, *inviting someone to a Bible program*, and *sharing the gospel.*

Distributing Religious Materials

Lily was excited! Her before-school Bible club had just started a couple of weeks ago. The group that was meeting together was on fire. They were a small group for now but were hoping to invite the rest of the student body to their meetings. Just this morning, the group had brainstormed some communication ideas like hanging posters, making a school-wide announcement, and giving out free Bibles. Lily was put in charge of figuring out some of the logistics for implementing these ideas. She decided to start by talking with her school principal.

Lily knew her principal had a full schedule, so rather than just show up at his office unannounced, she sent him an email introducing the topic of discussion and respectfully requesting a meeting time that would fit his schedule and information about school policies on distributing religious materials. He agreed, and Lily made sure she prepared everything she needed him to review: a draft of the announcement and the poster, and one of the Bibles to be given away.

When Lily met with the principal, she thanked him for meeting with her. She then shared about the Bible club that had been meeting and conveyed their desire to invite the rest of the student body to join them. She shared their ideas for hanging the posters, making a school-wide announcement, and handing out the Bibles. The principal then shared the school's policies on where posters could be hung and for how long. He also guided her to include a phrase at the beginning of the announcement to clarify that the club was extending the invitation, not the school. He also shared some school guidelines on distributing materials. As the meeting ended, Lily thanked her principal again for his time and the information he shared. She left the meeting feeling good about the direction of the club's promotional strategy. It was in line with school policies, and the principal was respectfully informed.

Let's review how Lily handled her club's plan to distribute promotional materials at their school:

- *She inquired about school policies on distributing religious materials.* Most public schools have policies regarding when and where information not related to classroom activities can be distributed on school property. Knowing how to navigate within those policies is the first step in showing respect for school administrators and teachers.
- *She was prepared.* Lily brought drafts of the poster and announcement to the meeting to show that the group was serious about wanting to connect with the student body. She also communicated respect for the principal by making sure he wouldn't be taken by surprise. While the First

Amendment protects the right of students to share a message, they must also be aware of school policies they'll need to follow. For example, permission might be needed to hang posters, or announcements might need a disclaimer. In being prepared, Lily showed respect for her principal's time.

- *She was gracious.* Lily started and ended her meeting with the principal by thanking him for his time and the information he shared. Graciously expressing appreciation is essential for cultivating a positive relationship based on trust. If Lily—or her club—faces criticism in the future, she can draw on this positive relationship with her principal for support.

What a great example of treating authority figures with respect! Make sure your children understand that when they show respect for teachers and school administrators, they are imitating Jesus. And affirm them in this whenever you can!

Inviting Someone to a Bible Program

For a couple of weeks, Billy had been attending an off-campus Bible program during school hours. One day, his small-group leader encouraged every child to think about someone who didn't know Jesus yet and pray for that person. She also encouraged them to consider sharing Jesus with that person and inviting them to learn more. The small group brainstormed ideas that included inviting the person to church or their Bible program, or giving them a free Bible. Since Billy was praying for a friend who was also a classmate, he felt that inviting his friend to their Bible program was the best choice. So he grabbed a registration form for his friend's parents to sign.

As the end of the school day approached, Billy had some butterflies in his stomach. He had no idea how his friend would respond to the invitation. But he was determined to be courageous like Joshua, one of the Old Testament heroes Billy had heard about in his Bible program.

After the bell rang, Billy approached his friend and handed him the registration form. Then he shared about the fun he was having learning about the Bible and encouraged his classmate to consider attending. Billy instructed his friend to have his mom fill out the form and return it to their school. His friend said he would think about it and stuffed the invitation into his bag before heading out the door. Billy said a quick, silent prayer for his friend while he ran to catch his own bus home.

Let's see how well Billy did proactively inviting his friend to the Bible program:

- *He shared a "why" for the invitation.* Billy not only invited his classmate to a Bible program, but he also explained why he thought his friend should come. By sharing how much fun he was having as he learned about the Bible, Billy was giving his classmate an incentive to join him.
- *He had something tangible to share as a reminder.* Kids are kids, and information tends to get lost in the shuffle when it's communicated verbally. Having something tangible to share, whether it's a form, a postcard, or even a pencil with a website on it, helps bring the invitation back to memory. Billy gave his friend a registration form that his mom could fill out, which was not only a great reminder but would also save his friend the trouble of tracking one down.

- *He gave his friend instructions on what to do.* When Billy gave his friend the registration form, he also shared what his friend needed to do with it. That extra step significantly increased the chances that his classmate would follow through and actually register for the Bible program.

It's a privilege for our kids to invite someone from their public school to attend a program or club where they'll learn about Jesus and the Bible. It also takes courage! When our kids express a desire to reach out to someone in this way, we need to support them in taking this proactive step on their faith journeys.

Sharing the Gospel

Over the past few days, Lauren had been contemplating a conversation she'd had with a friend at school last week. As they discussed the topic of creating good habits, her friend dismissed the idea. "What does it matter?" she said. "We're all going to die anyway and cease existing, so we should just seize the day. After all, you only live once! Life is too overwhelming to worry about creating good habits. The important thing is having fun to relieve the stress."

But Lauren knew that God promised otherwise. Death was not the end; heaven was waiting for everyone who put their faith in Jesus Christ. The hopelessness her friend expressed bothered Lauren until she felt the need to say something.

Lauren had given her life to Jesus as a child and attended church and youth group faithfully. Yet she had never really spoken about her faith with anyone who wasn't a Christian. She felt that she should prepare for such an important conversation, so she turned to her youth-group leader for advice. With a few conversation points under her belt, she was ready.

One afternoon, as they walked home from school, Lauren brought up their discussion about what happens after death. She acknowledged her friend's feeling that sometimes life can be overwhelming, and having fun can ease the stress. Then Lauren shared that she also felt overwhelmed at times, but while fun had its place, it couldn't totally take away the empty feeling that only God could fill. She went on to tell her friend about Jesus and the gospel. The two girls talked at some length as Lauren tried her best to answer her friend's questions. She didn't know the answers to all of them, but she promised to find answers and get back to her.

Upon arriving home, Lauren took a moment to reflect on the conversation and jot down her friend's questions. She was hopeful that she could chat with her youth-group leader and then follow up with her friend. The experience wasn't the big salvation moment Lauren had thought it would be, but her friend was open to hearing more, and that encouraged her.

Let's review the steps Lauren took to proactively share her faith with a friend:

- *She built rapport.* By asking questions and listening, Lauren discovered she could identify with how overwhelmed her classmate felt sometimes. This opened the door for a more serious conversation.
- *She shared her faith confidently.* Lauren had prepared for this conversation, so she was able to confidently share her faith and explain why it was important to her.
- *She patiently accepted God's timing.* Deep down, Lauren had expected her friend to accept Jesus on the spot and be dazzled by her new faith. After all, it was the best news ever! But

when that didn't happen, Lauren recognized that this would unfold in God's timing, and she just needed to be patient and obedient in following up on the questions she needed to find answers for.

Handing your kids the keys to unlock the conversation tools they need to live out their faith at school can be fun. If they're up for it, acting out scenarios can be a joyful bonding time. Any time they have a reason to talk about Jesus, it's a good thing. Speaking truth in love and having discernment to know when to speak and when to stay silent are skills that require practice, especially in a public-school environment. So is giving godly responses when the comments or opinions of others collide with our kids' faith. It takes courage to use these conversation tools at school, but every interaction our children learn to navigate, with our support, will grow their faith and prepare them for the future.

There's one more essential supply for your kids' backpacks that they can't leave home without. But this one will require courage on your part. I can't wait to show you!

Just in Case

When asked why he kept his steps-to-salvation card in his desk at school, a little boy replied, "It's in my desk just in case someone wants to know about Jesus."

CHAPTER 14

ROLE MODELS ON SPEED DIAL

The van ride home from school was a noisy, boisterous one. Brenda, a stay-at-home mom and taxi driver for three energetic elementary-aged kids, smiled as she looked in the rearview mirror at her children laughing and teasing each other in the back seat. From the time their kids were infants, Brenda and her husband made the intentional decision to pour God's Word into them and disciple them. Their family belonged to a vibrant church, and the kids were involved in a variety of Bible programs. When Brenda and her husband chose a public-school education for their children, they made sure their kids knew they could live out their faith at school, just as they did at home. Brenda even signed the kids up for a dynamic released-time Bible program held during the school day.

But like most parents, she had one lingering concern: her children's friend choices. She knew how important it was for them to have godly friends on their faith journeys, and yet that wasn't a guarantee in public school. Proverbs 13:20 rang in her mind: "Whoever walks with the wise becomes wise, but the companion of fools will suffer harm." Her kids had nice friends, but not all of them were believers. Brenda began to pray specifically for her oldest son—not just that he would walk with wise friends but also that those who didn't come from homes of faith would have the opportunity to meet Jesus through him.

Sometimes your children's public-school classes will be filled with believers and great friend choices. When that's the case, praise the Lord! In reality, however, it's possible your children won't be able to identify even one other child who comes from a Christian home. Shockingly, according to the 2022 *American Worldview Inventory*, an annual survey conducted by the Cultural Research Center at Arizona Christian University, "Only 2% of . . . parents [of preteens in the United States] emerge as adults with a biblical worldview." And fewer than 20 percent of them attended a Bible-believing church.[1] As dismal as those statistics sound, they don't necessarily indicate an unwillingness to learn about Jesus from adults who care about their families.

Brenda cared deeply about her son and his new friends. She encouraged her boy to invite his friend Riley, who didn't have a church home, to his released-time Bible program, Bible2School. Though he loved the program, her son confessed that he felt too nervous to ask Riley. He didn't want to seem pushy or call attention to their differences. Her son wasn't shy about his Christian faith, but he lacked experience when it came to reaching out to lost people. Brenda realized she needed to teach her kids about Jesus' heart for their friends. They needed to know how to stand as followers of Jesus and be witnesses to others in school. *But what's the best way to teach them?* she wondered.

As Brenda sought the Lord for direction, the answer became clear. She needed to take a brave step of her own. *Don't just tell them how to live their faith,* she thought. *Show them! Be their role model!* So that's exactly what she did.

I've found that this scenario isn't unique. Many Christian parents and their children have never shared the gospel with those around them. It would seem that the average American hasn't lived alongside true, biblically minded, Christ-following disciples of Jesus who have a heart for lost people. Can you think of someone who models this heart for the lost and shares the gospel as well? Are you one of those people? Being asked tough questions like these can be a little uncomfortable.

Imitating Jesus requires work, and being real-life examples of faith for our children requires courage. As parents, we need to get off the bleachers and live out our faith in the world! If this generation is truly lacking parental role models who know and understand the Word of God, we've received our call to action. The need constitutes the call. We need to not only be our kids' role models; we also need to find other trusted adult role models to invest in our children's faith walk.

This isn't impossible. In fact, I've watched hundreds of parents get off the bleachers and step onto the field of soul-winning, engaged, and dynamic faith.

In this chapter, we'll look at the seventh essential backpack supply: *an emergency contact card of adult role models.* This card is an important reminder that even though our children may be in the minority when they walk through the doors of their public school, they are not alone.

Emergency Contact Card (of Adult Role Models)

I don't know about you, but one of my least favorite things to do during the first week of school is fill out school forms. Although necessary and important, it seems like I fill out the same information over and over as my pen makes its way through the stack of forms. Now that my youngest has graduated from college, I've heard that these forms are *finally* being digitized for families. Consider yourself blessed! Although these forms contain information schools need, few are more important than your children's emergency contact information.

The emergency contact cards in your children's faith backpacks include all the numbers a school or coach needs to reach you in case of an emergency. Also listed are the names of adult family members or friends you trust to step in and make important decisions for any of your children if you can't be reached. So an emergency contact card helps your child always have the contact information for the most trusted adults in his or her life. In addition to being emergency contacts, these adults may also be role models your children trust that you hope they'll want to emulate.

As their beloved parents, you are your kids' primary role models, their go-to people. But having this team of backup role models is necessary. As a mom of three grown children, I can tell you from experience, a solid team of adult role models is a powerful force in kids' lives, not just when they get sick at school, but when they need spiritual guidance and life-on-life mentoring.

WHAT DOES BEING A ROLE MODEL LOOK LIKE?

I know the concept of being an adult role model for a child sounds daunting. As a matter of fact, few adults on our family's emergency contact list have ever been asked if they would provide this kind of mentorship for our kids. Few of us want to be held to a higher standard, and we rarely think we're worthy of being imitated. But kids are watching us all the time, even when we think they aren't, so we're often serving as role models whether we realize it or not. The worrisome part is that we know we aren't perfect. We're well acquainted with all the ways we fall short.

But here's an important news flash: *You don't have to be a perfect person to be a good role model for your kids.* You just need to be willing to live out your faith in the little and big moments of life, seeking to imitate Jesus as the Holy Spirit works in you. Simply put, being a positive role model means you walk closely beside your children, teaching them through your words and actions how a man or woman who loves God behaves, regardless of the situation.

In 1 Corinthians 11:1, the apostle Paul tells us, "Follow my example, as I follow the example of Christ" (NIV). Can you imagine boldly saying something like that to anyone? "Do it like I do it, because I'm following Jesus!" That is what Paul did, and he instructs us to do the same: "Be imitators of God, as beloved children" (Ephesians 5:1). Jesus is the ultimate role model we need to emulate for our kids.

Interestingly, research indicates that about 65 percent of people identify as visual learners.[2] I'm one of them. Showing me how to do something is a much faster way for me to learn than just telling me verbally. I have to see it to truly understand it. About 85 percent of school-age children are visual learners as well.[3]

One of the things I love most about our heavenly Father is that He didn't just *tell* us how to live a life pleasing to Him; He showed us! God sent His precious Son, Jesus, to earth to rescue us from sin and show us how to love Him and others well.

I'm sure you're wondering how to model a life of faith for the children God has given you. This is off-the-bleachers thinking! As we jump in, let's glean some practical applications from Jesus' life.

WHAT DID JESUS DO?

During His time here on earth, Jesus showed us, in uncomplicated ways, how to please God as we live out our faith. As our role model, Jesus knew how important it was to stay close to His heavenly Father, and the way He spent His time reflected this goal. A wise friend told me, "No matter how busy people are, they make time for what is important to them." Jesus couldn't accomplish His Father's mission without a deep connection with Him. Of course, the same is true for us. To stay refreshed and aligned with His Father's will, Jesus prioritized His time in three ways: *He spent time alone with God*, *He spent time serving others*, and *He spent time connecting with believers.*

He Spent Time Alone with God

Jesus made it a priority to spend time alone with His Father. He got up early in the morning and went away by Himself to pray (Mark 1:35). Through prayer, Jesus sought the Father's will above all else. This time brought renewal, clarity, alignment, and strength. You may be thinking, *What would it look like to fit time alone with God into my already overflowing day?*

It doesn't need to be complicated. Time alone with God can be just talking to Him while you drink a cup of coffee, read Scripture, and pray before your kids get up in the morning. It could be taking five minutes to pray in your car in the parking lot of your workplace or on your way home from dropping off the kids at school. It could be reading your Bible at your kitchen counter before planning your day. Or meditating on the Bible verses stuck to your bathroom mirror as you blow-dry your hair. It could mean listening to worship music while you try to meet that ten-thousand-step goal.

Time with the Lord can happen at any time of the day or night. Jesus talked to His Father often. He valued knowing the Scriptures and relied on them to articulate truth to others. Intentionally nurturing a good habit of prayer and Bible reading will not only fill you up with God's Spirit, but it will also show your kids how to live a life that makes a relationship with God their top priority.

I recently found out from my daughter-in-law exactly how much my kids were watching and catching from me as they were growing up. I shared with her that when my boys were young, I had a habit of praying for them every morning before they rose. I also wouldn't let them leave the house for school until I whispered a five-second prayer in their ears as I hugged them goodbye.

Her eyes brightened and she smiled. "That explains it! Every morning your son won't leave the house until we pray together. Sometimes he just waits by the sink in the bathroom until I'm done brushing my teeth. And then we pray before either of us leaves the house. It's really sweet!"

Role-modeling Jesus really can be as simple as establishing godly habits and sticking with them. I can't wait to hear how your kids catch you prioritizing your relationship with Jesus, and how it impacts their lives over time. Just like yeast kneaded into flour, time proves its presence and changes everything.

He Spent Time Serving Others

Jesus came to earth to humbly serve others. He literally surrendered His own will and laid down His life to bring us to God. Jesus said, "The Son of Man came not to be served but to serve, and to give his life as a ransom for many" (Matthew 20:28).

Jesus valued people and prioritized serving them. He talked to people from all walks of life and built relationships with them. He taught them and answered their questions; He healed the sick and fed people who were hungry; He performed miracles and raised people from the dead. He invested His time, talent, and treasure in people and ultimately gave His life for us.

We can't be like Jesus unless we serve others and model servanthood for our kids. Jesus emphasized two essential ways we can serve others:

1. *Physically.* Jesus embodied the gospel message in His actions, meeting the physical needs of others and giving us an example to follow. When we feed the hungry, clothe the naked, help strangers, and visit those who are sick or in prison, Jesus says we're doing these things to Him (Matthew 25:31-40). As God brings those who need help across our paths, we can model for our kids how to serve others by meeting their physical needs.
2. *Spiritually.* Jesus also met the spiritual needs of others by sharing the message of salvation. This is what He has commanded us to do: "Therefore, go and make disciples of all the nations, baptizing them in the name of the Father and the Son and the Holy Spirit. Teach these new disciples to obey all the commands I have given you" (Matthew 28:19-20, NLT). When we lead others to Jesus by sharing the gospel with them, we're following His example and teaching our kids to do the same.

Being a Christlike role model for your children in the public-school system requires a spirit of humility and a servant's heart. Look for ways to serve others together. Leading by example can have a powerful influence on your children. Model what it looks like to serve family members, friends, neighbors, your school, and your community using the gifts God has given you. It's time well spent for both you and your children.

He Spent Time Connecting with Believers

Jesus connected with people and had real relationships with them. He knew their strengths and character flaws, and He even gave them nicknames, like calling James and John the "Sons of Thunder" (Mark 3:17). He discerningly chose twelve men as His disciples and invested deeply in their lives. He shared meals with them, encouraged them, and prayed for them. As the number of believers grew, Jesus regularly carved out time alone with His disciples to strengthen them. Their companionship undoubtedly encouraged Him as well.

After rising from the dead, Jesus instructed His disciples to gather together and wait for the promised Holy Spirit (Acts 1:4-5). When Jesus returned to His Father, we find the disciples gathered, praying together with Jesus' mother, Mary; the women who followed Him; and His brothers (verses 12-14). It's interesting that Jesus had them remain together, isn't it? There is strength in numbers, and Jesus was about to do a brand-new work in and through them. They would need one another for the days ahead. And we need one another too.

Jesus modeled how to live in community with fellow believers, how to disciple others, and how to be a Christlike friend who is patient and kind and speaks the truth in love. God knew we weren't created to be alone; we were created to do life in community.

The author of Hebrews reminds us,

> Let us hold fast the confession of our hope without wavering, for he who promised is faithful. And let us consider how to stir up one another to love and good works, not neglecting to meet together, as is the habit of some, but encouraging one another, and all the more as you see the Day drawing near.
>
> HEBREWS 10:23-25

Did you notice the "one anothers" in this passage? We need to remember we can't "one another" without another person, and we can't do it well without being together. Jesus showed us how vital life-on-life training is for building up each other's faith. Spending time connecting with other believers is essential for our mutual encouragement and spiritual growth. Let's show our kids what that looks like!

Now that we have a clearer idea of what it means to be a Christlike role model for our kids, let's consider the other role models on their emergency contact card. We carefully choose these trusted people while our kids are in school, and as they mature, we teach them how to find their own trustworthy role models.

FIVE TRUSTED ROLE MODELS

Sticky Faith, a fascinating book by Dr. Kara Powell and Dr. Chap Clark, is a Christian-parenting favorite.[4] Concerned about the statistics showing that kids often leave their faith when they head to college, Powell and Clark have researched how faith can become "sticky," capturing kids' hearts for Jesus for a lifetime. They deftly explain the importance of creating a "sticky web" of at least five trusted adults who will positively support, mentor, and be adult role models for our children in their faith walk.[5] While it's possible to remain grounded in their faith alone, whenever possible our children must invite others into their journeys. Powell and Clark encourage intentionally cultivating and creating this "sticky web" by identifying family members, friends, coaches, church members, and neighbors who are believers and are willing to do life with our children and our families. These godly adult role models should welcome your children, root for them, pray for them, give them feedback when asked, spend time with them, and make them feel valued.

Role models are so important! The environment we surround our kids with has a direct impact on who they become and the way they behave. So putting intentional mentors in their paths matters. Quality mentoring relationships have powerful positive effects on young people in a variety of personal, academic, and professional situations. Positive role models can also protect our kids from engaging in high-risk behaviors, including violence, sex outside marriage, and substance abuse.

In *Making a Difference: An Impact Study of Big Brothers Big Sisters*, we see the impact that positive role models can have in our children's lives:

- Forty-six percent of kids who have positive role models in their lives are less likely than their peers to start using illegal drugs.
- Twenty-seven percent of kids with mentors are less likely to start drinking.[6]

Meanwhile, "85% of young people with a mentor say this key relationship has helped them with issues related to school and their education."[7]

In different seasons of their lives, our kids are going to look to other people for guidance, support, and answers to some big life questions. This is a healthy and good desire, so it's imperative that while our children are young, we help them cultivate a network of godly role models they trust.

CHOOSING ADULT ROLE MODELS FOR YOUR CHILD

One summer, a heavy life problem unfolded and overtook my oldest son like a dark cloud. Several of his friends were involved in a difficult conflict with each other, and unfortunately, my son was stuck in the middle. At a loss over how to handle the bleak situation, my son came to us for advice. He also sought out a good friend of my husband's—I'll call him Tom—for wisdom and insight. Tom was one of the five or six adult role models who invested consistently in my boy's life through the years. After gleaning much wisdom from Tom in a long conversation, my son got off the phone feeling lighter.

My husband asked, "What did Tom say?"

My son shared, "He gave me good advice that really lined up with what you've told me, Dad. In fact, he said that you are the smartest person he knows, and that I should pray over the situation and listen to your wisdom."

Tom's willingness to be an available mentor was a priceless gift. My husband and I were so thankful that we prioritized developing and sustaining positive adult role models for our kids. It was an added bonus, of course, that Tom made my husband look like a hero. In reality, Tom's opinion on how to handle something didn't need to match ours. Scripture is clear that "there is safety in having many advisers" (Proverbs 11:14, NLT). The real prize is knowing that Tom pointed our son to the ultimate source of wisdom, his heavenly Father.

Choosing positive adult role models who are godly believers is not as challenging as you might think. In fact, the first place to look for these candidates could be the "favorites" list on your cell phone. As you scroll through this list, ask yourself, *Why do I like this person? Would I want my kids to have them on their speed dial?*

Our kids are precious cargo, and we naturally want what is safest and best for them. So let's talk about a few of the attributes a trusted adult role model should have:

- *Genuineness.* Being genuine is highly valued in our day. It means to be authentic, trustworthy, transparent, real, and reliable. A genuine person's outward actions will align with their inward disposition. As parents, we want genuine role models for our children who will tell it like it is and aren't afraid of the messiness that sometimes comes with trying to live a life of faith.
- *Availability.* While being busy seems to be a cultural merit badge, availability is rare and precious. Being available to your child means being willing and able to make space and time for a relationship with them. It also means being committed to communicating with your child in supportive and uplifting ways in person and through other means, such as texting, email, and even traditional mail. In our fast-paced culture, being available, whether emotionally or physically, stands out as a beautiful gift to your child.

- *Mentoring.* Mentors give advice and training to those in their care. Mentoring can involve sitting and talking with a child, or it could take place in an active setting. A mentoring relationship can and should be as unique as the two individuals involved. The one thing that should be present, however, is wisdom. Whoever mentors your child must be willing to listen closely and then share godly wisdom. Of course, no one has all the answers, but the Bible tells us that God will give us wisdom if we ask for it (James 1:5). That's great news!
- *A heart for encouraging others.* Nothing feels better to kids than encouragement from someone who cares about them. Catching them doing something good and commenting on it can mean more to kids than visiting an all-you-can-eat ice-cream parlor. Encouragement involves affirming skill sets, behaviors, actions, and attitudes. From high fives to notes of encouragement and phone calls to regular texts sharing Scripture or affirmations, encouragement is inexpensive but valuable. Getting this type of affirmation from a respected adult role model can be life-changing for your child.

The best role models for our children are those who walk with Jesus. If we desire a growing, dynamic faith walk for our children, then a believer will be the best person to teach them. But there are times when a nonbeliever of upstanding and honorable character will step into our children's lives and naturally become one of their role models. Our sons have had coaches and neighbors who have invested in their lives and our family.

If you think a nonbeliever would be a good role model for your child, take time to talk through the admirable qualities of this person and pray for their salvation together.

While watching these "sticky" relationships grow and develop, keep adding relevant people to that web. Does your child have a special interest in the outdoors? Then work to cultivate relationships with men or women who do as well. Is your child musical? Try to find a musician who will point your child to Jesus through their music. Are you raising a kid who loves to read? Then take time to find someone who would love to talk about good books. Remember, good role models will come in all shapes and sizes, but like our friend Tom, who spoke into our son's life, they will point our kids to Jesus and back home as their safe place.

Your home will likely be a safe place for your child's friends as well, providing a welcome respite as they sense Jesus in your midst. The best relationships grow organically, so don't forget when they run in and out of the house that you are representing Christ in a special way. In your home, at your dinner table, or snuggled on your couch, your kids and their friends will share their hearts with you naturally. It's a great time to be one of those safe speed-dial people who talk about Jesus and how much He loves them.

GO FIRST: THE REST OF BRENDA'S STORY

Remember Brenda's concern at the beginning of this chapter? She'd taken a quick glance at the kids surrounding her son and realized there weren't a lot of believers in the mix. Like most Christian parents, she longed for her son to know the fellowship and faith-strengthening community of having Christian friends. Brenda encouraged her son to invite his friend Riley to join him at his Bible2School program, but he felt too nervous to ask. After all, it was rather scary to start the conversation, and she could empathize.

So Brenda prayed for wisdom and courage. She decided to get

off the bleachers and model what an invitation to friends looks like. She had chatted with Riley's mom at a few school events, so she thought, *Why don't I show my son how to invite someone to a Christian event, even if it makes me feel uncomfortable? With the right words and the right heart posture, Riley's mom might welcome an invitation, even if she doesn't take me up on it.*

Brenda texted Riley's mom and invited Riley to the Bible2School program. In case that wasn't preferable, she also extended an invitation to their family to join them at church on Sunday. Riley's mom chose the latter. Imagine the joy Brenda and her son felt as they greeted Riley and his family at their church the following Sunday. People won't always accept our invitations, but Brenda did something impactful. She modeled to her son how to trust God and live out her faith in the community. And it was powerful.

Be a role model for your children. Create a mentoring atmosphere and surround them with adults who will live out their faith in front of them. Not only will your children grow deeper roots spiritually, but you and your tribe of friends will grow too!

"God Is Real"

Kli Kli felt awkward as the new kid in her second-grade class. She had just arrived from Thailand and didn't know the language very well. She didn't know about Jesus either, so she signed up for a Bible2School program. Her leader, whom she called "Mr. Roger," was kind and made her feel comfortable and accepted. He taught her that God loves her and has a plan and purpose for her life. What seemed to surprise Kli Kli the most was that Mr. Roger lived and shared that God is real.[8]

CHAPTER 15

IT'S TIME TO GET IN THE GAME!

Thunder boomed as rain pelted the metal roof of the yellow school bus, creating a steady drumming sound. Sharing a green vinyl seat, Annie and two of her friends, McKenna and Sarah, put their heads down and plugged their ears. With just a look, the three communicated to one another their common feeling of fear. It was the loudest storm nine-year-old Annie had ever heard. The bus driver attempted to soothe the bus full of frazzled children by urging them to lower their voices.

Sitting between her friends on the padded seat, Annie decided to fold her hands, close her eyes, and pray quietly. She was raised with a strong faith in Jesus and accepted Him as her Savior when she was young. Annie knew Jesus could help calm her in her moment of need. McKenna, also a believer, closed her eyes and folded her hands, joining Annie in silent prayer to God to "let the storm go away." Sarah, who wasn't a believer, eyed her friends sideways in the seat with a puzzled look.

As quickly as the violent storm started, it passed, and the girls breathed a sigh of relief. McKenna waved to her friends as she exited the bus at the next stop.

After McKenna left, Sarah asked Annie, "What were you guys doing?"

Annie told her, "We were praying."

Sarah replied, "What's that?"

Annie shared, "That's when we talk to God, who made the whole world and us, too. We love Him and He loves us, and we can talk to Him anytime. When we pray, we ask Him stuff or tell Him stuff. I was telling God I felt afraid and asked Him to please stop the storm and keep us safe."

Sarah said, "Oh wow! That sounds really cool. I wish I had somebody I could do that with."

Annie shared, "Oh, you do. You can talk to God too!"

For the rest of the bus ride, Annie was able to tell Sarah about her Savior, Jesus, who died on the cross for their sins. She told her that Jesus rose from the dead and that they could be in heaven with Him someday, if they prayed to Him.

Sarah said, "I want to do that."

So Annie had the privilege of leading her friend through a prayer of salvation, a decision that impacted Sarah eternally. Both girls were thrilled!

That night, Annie shared what happened on the bus with her mom, and the next day she brought Sarah a Bible. Sarah was so grateful to her friend and was eager to learn about God. In fact, the following week, Sarah told Annie that her mom loved to read her new Bible to her every night. It was a new favorite routine for both of them.

Isn't that the best? It really is possible for children to lead others in steps of faith. God opened the door, and little Annie knew what to do: point her friend to Jesus. Only heaven will reveal all the little moments that led to Sarah's incredible moment of salvation. Surely the everyday conversations Annie's parents had with her about faith mattered in this moment and will continue making an impact in the years that will follow. Annie's parents took their role seriously as their daughter's disciplers. They sowed seeds of faith in her life, and fruit followed. Not only was this fruit seen in Annie's life, but seeds were planted in Sarah's and her mom's lives too. Right there on that public-school bus, God used a little girl for His glory.

We want that for our children. God wants that for them too.

To help your children live out their faith in public school, like Annie, there is one more nugget of wisdom I hope you will consider. It may be the most countercultural decision you'll make.

Buckle up! This nugget of wisdom will likely feel convicting, and it involves your family calendar.

THE CALENDAR LITMUS TEST

We're all busy. Our calendars tend to brim, possibly slosh over, much of the time.

It's important to recognize that "busy" certainly affects our children and their spiritual development. There are two types of busy: healthy and unhealthy. Healthy busy for kids involves things that enrich their growth, such as going to church, regular doctor appointments, and playdates with quality friends; spending time with adult role models; and participating in music lessons or a sport. But when busyness squeezes God out of our children's lives, it becomes unhealthy.

One study estimates that the average adolescent spends 7.9 hours participating in extracurricular activities per week, 9.1 hours per week doing homework, and 2.5 evenings per week hanging out with peers.[1] That's on top of their full six- to eight-hour school day. Ever-growing cultural pressure seems to invoke in parents the fear that their kids will miss out on opportunities. A plethora of extracurricular activities, sometimes happening simultaneously, along with overflowing social commitments, tend to take priority in our children's lives. When this happens, their discipleship is often demoted to an afterthought.

How did we let our kids' schedules get so packed? Well, if you find yourself in this predicament, don't beat yourself up too much. Our culture thrives on being busy. It's even become a badge of honor for our kids to engage in extra activities. Club sports, honors programs, and even church events vie for their attention. Like getting caught up in the current of a river, families can get swept up in overflowing schedules. As keepers of our calendars, we find that busyness often sneaks up on us. We may have good intentions, but like everything else in parenting, we have to be strategic if we want to ensure that discipleship happens in our family. It's vital to consistently make sure our children are learning about God and the Bible and investing in growing their faith. How can we ensure this happens?

It all comes down to time management—how we, as parents, teach our children to use the gift of time. If you're like me, every opportunity feels important. So I end up saying yes to everything. Consequently, my family suffers with very little margin, and our good intentions take a back seat to the urgent. Stephen Covey, acclaimed author of *The Seven Habits of Highly Effective People*, says, "*The key is not to prioritize what's on your schedule, but to schedule your priorities.*"[2]

Prioritizing time with God matters, and so does modeling it

for our children. Putting God first is an excellent life lesson for kids that, if taught when they're young, can develop into a lifelong pattern. Jesus said, "Let the little children come to me, and do not hinder them, for the kingdom of heaven belongs to such as these" (Matthew 19:14, NIV). When we fill our children's schedules to the brim, we may be hindering them from spending quality time with God. Over time, this will teach them, whether we mean to or not, that He is *not* the highest priority in their lives. Nothing could be further from the truth!

My husband and I realized when our boys were young that time goes by quickly, and we can't get it back. We found that unless we were intentional with our time, the boys' discipleship wouldn't happen. So we decided to implement a calendar litmus test involving a series of questions that would help us guard our family's calendar and keep God as our top priority. We found these questions invaluable for decision-making, and we still use a similar method today.

The litmus test we currently use for evaluating opportunities for our children's calendars is called the Good, Better, Best Calendar Test. When an opportunity came up for one of our kids, we would say, "It's all good, but what is better, and what is *best* for our child and our family?" We would add to the calendar only what we deemed best for our child, even if that meant saying no to good things. We called this a "good no." It was a hard but good decision to eliminate busyness for the benefit of our child.

This litmus test made us prioritize well. In some seasons, our calendars would get too full, and we would need to self-correct with a few good noes. But each week, we determined what was best for our children and taught them to do the same in the context of our family's goals and seasons.

Helping kids prioritize time spent with God in their schedules is not only best; it's biblical! The Bible has a lot to say about how to prioritize our time wisely. Consider the following Scripture passages in light of your calendar today:

- "'Seek the Kingdom of God above all else, and live righteously, and he will give you everything you need'" (Matthew 6:33, NLT).
- "Do not conform to the pattern of this world, but be transformed by the renewing of your mind. Then you will be able to test and approve what God's will is—his good, pleasing and perfect will" (Romans 12:2, NIV).
- "Be very careful, then, how you live—not as unwise but as wise, making the most of every opportunity, because the days are evil" (Ephesians 5:15-16, NIV).

Keeping your family calendar aligned with the Bible means that you, the adult, must pull yourself up above the chaos and set your sights on a healthy, Spirit-filled perspective of your calendar and spiritual goals. How you and your children spend the precious gift of time in this season will affect their spiritual development. Here are some things my husband and I considered when testing prospective activities for our children (see the appendix to find more questions):

- *Will this activity help them grow in their walk with God?*
- *Will this activity cultivate edifying friendships?*
- *Are healthy role models involved in this activity?*
- *Will this activity disrupt scheduled Bible reading or prayer time?*
- *Does this activity align with the season our family is in?*

Regardless of the season you are in as a parent, there is no better way to spend your time than intentionally discipling your children. If you get nothing else from this book, I want you to know that investing your time in discipling your kids truly impacts them. It will always be time well spent.

READY TO GET IN THE GAME?

The moments you spend filling your children's faith backpacks with the seven essential supplies we've unpacked in this book will prepare them to get off the sidelines and into the game. They'll be well equipped to walk through the doors of public school with confidence, and you will be confident too, knowing that you have fulfilled your God-given assignment. The truth is that although we don't know the conversations and lessons that lie ahead for our children, we can say with confidence that God will be with them every step of the way.

While it may be tempting to only ask God to protect your kids, I pray you now know in your heart that a life of spiritual courage packaged within the unique design of each child is possible. With this in mind, I have one last encouraging story to share with you from a public-school teacher. In a recent interview on our Bible2School podcast, this woman of God described how one fifth-grade boy with a well-stocked backpack influenced his entire class:

> One day, a little boy in my class was reading a small New Testament. I thought, *Wow, that's amazing! Right here in the middle of class, he's reading Scripture!* So I asked him about it, and he said the little Bible was given to him by a classmate. In fact, that classmate led him to

> Christ in the cafeteria and then gave him a Bible of his own.
>
> What I didn't realize at the time was that his classmate kept a supply of five Bibles in his backpack at all times, so he was always prepared to hand one out when God showed him someone who needed His Holy Word. Bible after Bible kept showing up on desktops in my classroom. Kids were reading the Bible in their free time. It was amazing. Children knew that this classmate would give them Bibles and explain the Word of God to them, so they sought him out. One day this classmate ran out of Bibles and gave away his own copy because he knew his mom would replenish his supply. I was moved to tears!

That's the good stuff, friend. When people ask if children's faith can survive public school, I can unequivocally shout, "Yes!" I've seen third graders lead their teachers in spiritual discussions. I've seen second graders lead their friends to Christ. I've heard about entire classrooms doing their book reports on the Bible. Yes, it's possible for your kids to live out their faith in public school and *thrive*!

So as you watch them run out the door with their backpacks bobbing up and down, filled with all the supplies they need, remember that God has *not* been taken out of public school. No authority in heaven or on earth has the power to keep God from any place. This includes the schools your children attend!

You know the law. You have the tools you need. You're equipped to get in the game. And God hears your prayers. He is working in a powerful way *in* public schools.

I can't wait to see how you choose to join Him as you and your children get in the game—living out your faith confidently, impacting others in *your* public school.

The Coach has called your name. It's time to get in the game! Now go for it!

ACKNOWLEDGMENTS

Ministry is a team sport, and so was this book project. So I would like to acknowledge and express my gratitude to the following.

The Holy Spirit, who led this project and continues to do so.

To my awesome writing team: Stephanie Smith, Megan Risser, Lee Neinhuis, and Kristi Tatro, thank you for your vital contributions to this project. You are incredibly talented and godly leaders. What a privilege it has been to grow and do Kingdom work with you on this adventure!

Bible2School National Board and Ambassador Teams: I am so grateful for your leadership and support in this project. May we continue to further grow awareness of our mission to glorify God.

I'm grateful to Erica Ringler, Shawna Ciampanelli, Liz Epright, Katlin Miller, Carol Rabold, Meredith Steidler, and the rest of our Bible2School staff. Thank you for your steadfast prayers and support.

To Jocelyn Hrovath, Stacy Novak, Gwen Marinaro, and the Bible2School Member Team: Thank you for continuing to inspire me as you teach public-school children about Jesus every week and share your "God stories" with me.

To Gabriel, Colson, Ivy, and Lydia: Your young, courageous faith always encourages me.

To Terri, Esther and Tim, Tina and Ron, Amy and Phil, Bonnie and Dave, Nikki and Doug, Donna and Roger, Deb and Jeff, Mark, Carla, Cheri, Elli, and our Bible2School National Prayer Warrior Team, you are the friends and prayer warriors who have poured into me and my children along the way. Thank you!

To my parents and my parents-in-law who, through their wonderful example, taught me to put God first. Thank you!

Thank you to the generous, grace-filled contributors and supporters who took the time to teach me and encourage me on this journey:

- Alex and Christina Kendrick, Kendrick Brothers Productions
- Peter Greer, HOPE International
- Joshua Enck and Matthew Neff, Sight & Sound Theatres
- Allon Lefever, author of *Launching the Entrepreneur Ship*
- Sarah Rivette, former editor of *The Washington Times*
- Billy Hallowell, CBN News
- Dr. Jennifer Rivera, Answers in Genesis
- Dr. Jerry Pattengale, Museum of the Bible
- Sally Burke, Moms in Prayer International
- Sara Murphy, Sight & Sound Theatres
- John Bomberger, former CEO of Choice Books
- Ryan Bomberger, The Radiance Foundation
- Ken Ham, Answers in Genesis
- Blythe Daniel, The Blythe Daniel Agency
- Jim Daly, Larry Weeden, Vance Fry, and the rest of the team at Focus on the Family
- Emerson Collins, Bring Your Bible to School Day
- Matt Sharp, Alliance Defending Freedom
- Grant Atkinson, Alliance Defending Freedom

- Randall Wenger, The Pennsylvania Family Institute
- Jeremy Samek, Esq., Independence Law Center
- First Liberty Institute
- Amanda Banks, Family Policy Alliance
- Dr. George Barna, The Barna Group
- Dr. Adam Rasmussen, Arizona Christian University
- Jack Terrell, KiDs Beach Club
- Joel Penton, LifeWise Academy
- Mike Harrell, BibLit
- Lisa Kilgore, Child Evangelism Fellowship of Lancaster
- Cindy Bultema, Bultema Impact Group (BIG)

APPENDIX

BACKPACK FAITH RESOURCES

My hope is that *Backpack Faith* has given you plenty of information and added confidence to help you guide your children toward living their faith in public school. At Bible2School, we've learned that parents are more likely to act when given a clear game plan and easy-to-use resources to help them execute that plan. So we've created some downloadable tools for your family to use on this journey. Scan the QR code or visit bible2school.com/backpack-faith-resources to find these tools.

GOD WAS NOT *TAKEN OUT OF PUBLIC SCHOOLS*

Want to review the principles of this book in a condensed format? No problem! *God Was* Not *Taken out of Public Schools* is a twenty-two-page guide designed to educate parents and caretakers on how their children can confidently live out their faith in public school. With this guide, you'll learn to separate fact from fiction concerning the separation of church and state, understand what a public school's proper role is when it comes to religious freedom, and review the most common rights that families have to express their faith within a school setting.

QUICK-REFERENCE GUIDES

These print-friendly lists will help your family review the ways you're able to freely live out your faith—every day and in every classroom. You'll find separate "Bill of Rights" downloads for Christian students and teachers as well as our "Religious Liberties in Public School" list of the essential religious freedoms available to your child in public school. Additionally, the one-page "Backpack of Faith Supplies" is a handy, accessible graphic that will remind your family of the seven essential supplies your children need to help them live out their faith.

Post a copy of one of these resources in a place where you'll see it at the beginning of every school day.

TOOLS FOR WORKING WITH TEACHERS

Sample Email to Request a Meeting

Not sure how to start a tough conversation with a teacher or school administrator? Sometimes all you need is a few words to get you started. Based on Alicia's story in chapter 11, our meeting-request email template makes it easy to copy, paste, and tweak the language to align with your specific situation.

"The ABCs of Kindly Educating Educators"

This is a simple graphic to help you remember the effective communication approach discussed in chapter 12.

Meeting Talking Points

These talking points, based on the ABCs of Kindly Educating, will help you feel confident and equipped as you head into a meeting with any educator. These talking points are based on Alicia's story in chapter 11, but they can be tweaked to fit your situation.

Good, Better, Best Starting Point Questions

Most of the opportunities that vie for a slot on your family's calendar are good, but what is better—and what is *best*—for your child and your family? It's fine to say no to some opportunities, and these questions will help you as you discern which ones.

GROUP DISCUSSION GUIDE

This guide is designed to be experienced in a group setting, no matter the size. We provide you with thoughtful questions, key insights, and practical prompts that spark conversation and real-life application. You will leave the group discussion feeling inspired and equipped to implement the key points discussed in this book. Let this be your road map to help you get off the bleachers and into the game.

NOTES

CHAPTER 1 | YOU'RE THE STARTER

1. George Barna, *Raising Spiritual Champions: Nurturing Your Child's Heart, Mind and Soul* (Arizona Christian University Press, 2023), cited in "CRC Research Shows US Preteens on Track to Abandon Biblical Christianity in Record Numbers," Cultural Research Center, Arizona Christian University, February 7, 2024, https://www.arizonachristian.edu/2024/02/07/us-preteens-on-track-to-abandon-biblical-christianity-in-record-numbers.
2. "Education," Gallup, accessed August 4, 2025, https://news.gallup.com/poll/1612/education.aspx.
3. "The Bill of Rights: A Transcription," America's Founding Documents, National Archives, last reviewed August 7, 2025, https://www.archives.gov/founding-docs/bill-of-rights-transcript.
4. Commission on Children at Risk, *Hardwired to Connect: The New Scientific Case for Authoritative Communities* (Institute for American Values, 2003): abstract by Kathleen Kovner Kline, NCJRS Virtual Library, 2003, https://www.ojp.gov/ncjrs/virtual-library/abstracts/hardwired-connect-new-scientific-case-authoritative-communities.
5. Commission on Children at Risk, *Hardwired to Connect*: abstract.
6. Daniel G. Whitney and Mark D. Peterson, "US National and State-Level Prevalence of Mental Health Disorders and Disparities of Mental Health Care Use in Children," *JAMA Pediatrics* 173, no. 4 (2019): 389–391, cited in "Mental Health by the Numbers," National Alliance on Mental Illness, updated 2025, https://www.nami.org/about-mental-illness/mental-health-by-the-numbers.
7. George Barna, "Worldview and Mental Health," chapel message at Arizona Christian University, January 18, 2024, cited at, "Loss of Biblical Worldview Fuels Mental Health Crisis Among Young Adults, Says CRC's

Barna," Arizona Christian University, January 28, 2024, https://www.arizonachristian.edu/2024/01/28/mental-health-crisis-among-young-adults-a-worldview-problem-says-crcs-barna.

CHAPTER 2 | UNDERSTANDING THE RULES OF THE GAME

1. Thomas Jefferson, "Jefferson's Letter to the Danbury Baptists," January 1, 1802, Library of Congress, https://www.loc.gov/loc/lcib/9806/danpre.html. Emphasis added.
2. "The Bill of Rights: A Transcription," America's Founding Documents, National Archives, last reviewed August 7, 2025, https://www.archives.gov/founding-docs/bill-of-rights-transcript.
3. "Minutes of the Board of Visitors of the University of Virginia, 7 October 1822," Founders Online, National Archives, https://founders.archives.gov/documents/Madison/04-02-02-0504.
4. Mark David Hall, "Faithful Citizenship: The Founders on Religion and the Republic," *Religion and Liberty* 30, no. 4 (October 23, 2020), https://www.acton.org/religion-liberty/volume-30-number-4/faithful-citizenship-founders-religion-and-republic.
5. "Guidance on Constitutionally Protected Prayer and Religious Expression in Public Elementary and Secondary Schools," US Department of Education, last reviewed January 14, 2025, https://www.ed.gov/laws-and-policy/laws-preschool-grade-12-education/preschool-grade-12-policy-documents/guidance-on-constitutionally-protected-prayer-and-religious-expression-in-public-elementary-and-secondary-schools.
6. Samuel James Smith, "The New-England Primer," *Britannica*, accessed March 4, 2019, https://www.britannica.com/topic/The-New-England-Primer.

CHAPTER 3 | EXPRESSING FAITH INDIVIDUALLY

1. Alliance Defending Freedom, *Student Rights Handbook, K–12 and University: A Guide to Constitutionally Protected Religious Freedom on Campus* (Alliance Defending Freedom, 2015), 3, https://assets.adflegal.org/archive/dl/2024-08/Student-Rights-Handbook.pdf.
2. Don Haddleton, "Thoughts on Prayer from Charles Spurgeon," *The Banner of Truth*, 2007, Christian Library, https://www.christianstudylibrary.org/article/thoughts-prayer-charles-spurgeon.
3. See the "About" page at First Liberty Institute's website, accessed September 19, 2025, https://firstliberty.org/about-us.
4. "Hannah Allen Case," First Liberty Institute, accessed August 15, 2025, https://firstliberty.org/cases/hannah-allen.

5. Benjamin Rush, *Essays, Literary, Moral and Philosophical*, 2nd ed. (Thomas and William Bradford, 1806), 93.
6. Woodrow Wilson, "The Bible and the Soldier," message to soldiers and sailors, August 1917, quoted in Albert Bushnell Hart, ed., *Selected Addresses and Public Papers of Woodrow Wilson* (Boni and Liveright, 1918), 218.
7. Alliance Defending Freedom, *Student Rights Handbook*, 8.
8. "SC School Lifts Ban on Religious Christmas Carols," Alliance Defending Freedom, November 25, 2013, https://adfmedia.org/press-release/sc-school-lifts-ban-religious-christmas-carols.
9. "Facts and Case Summary—Tinker v. Des Moines," 393 U.S. 503 (1969), United States Courts, accessed August 15, 2025, https://www.uscourts.gov/educational-resources/educational-activities/facts-and-case-summary-tinker-v-des-moines.

CHAPTER 4 | EXPRESSING FAITH WITH OTHERS

1. George Barna, "*American Worldview Inventory 2023*—Release #1: Incidence of Biblical Worldview Shows Significant Change Since the Start of the Pandemic," Cultural Research Center, Arizona Christian University, February 28, 2023, https://www.arizonachristian.edu/wp-content/uploads/2023/02/CRC_AWVI2023_Release1.pdf.
2. Billy Graham, "A Time for Moral Courage," *Reader's Digest*, July 1964.
3. Ryan Jenkins, "3 Things Making Gen Z the Loneliest Generation," *Psychology Today*, August 16, 2022, https://www.psychologytoday.com/us/blog/the-case-connection/202208/3-things-making-gen-z-the-loneliest-generation.
4. "Is Your Child Lonely? (For Parents)," accessed December 23, 2025, Mental Health America, https://mhanational.org/resources/is-your-child-lonely-for-parents.
5. Jean Twenge, "Teens Are Lonelier Than Ever. What Do Smartphones Have to Do with It?," Institute for Family Studies, August 10, 2021, https://ifstudies.org/blog/teens-are-lonelier-than-ever-what-do-smartphones-have-to-do-with-it.
6. "Free Speech in Schools: Lawsuit Filed; Christians in Action Club vs Mechanicsburg Area School District," Independence Law Center, January 31, 2019, https://independencelaw.org/masdfreespeech. See also "Case Page: Christians in Action Club v. Mechanicsburg Area School District," Independence Law Center, accessed August 16, 2025, https://independencelaw.org/christiansinaction.
7. "Clubs and Organizations," GHMS Clubs: FCS, Gerald G. Huesken Middle School, Conestoga Valley School District, accessed August 16, 2025, https://ghms.conestogavalley.org/for-students/clubs-organizations.

8. Benjamin Rush, "Education Agreeable to a Republican Form of Government," in *The Selected Writings of Benjamin Rush*, ed. Dagobert D. Runes (Philosophical Library, 1947), 97.

CHAPTER 5 | EXPRESSING FAITH IN CLASS AND AT SCHOOL EVENTS

1. Grant Atkinson, "Censorship Is Incompatible with a Free Society," Alliance Defending Freedom, November 8, 2023, https://adflegal.org/article/censorship-incompatible-free-society.
2. "Graduation Speech Rights," First Liberty Institute, accessed August 18, 2025, https://firstliberty.org/graduation-speech-rights.
3. Benjamin Franklin, "Silence Dogood, No. 8," *New-England Courant*, July 9, 1722, Founders Online, National Archives, https://founders.archives.gov/documents/Franklin/01-01-02-0015. Spelling and word treatment modernized for clarity.
4. "Poll: Majority of Americans Believe First Amendment Goes TOO FAR in the Rights It Guarantees," FIRE, August 1, 2024, https://www.thefire.org/news/poll-majority-americans-believe-first-amendment-goes-too-far-rights-it-guarantees. "The new poll, conducted July 5-10, is the latest installment in the National Speech Index, a quarterly survey designed by FIRE and the Polarization Research Lab at Dartmouth College."
5. Samuel Adams, "The Rights of the Colonists," in *The Writings of Samuel Adams, Volume II, 1770–1773*, ed. Harry Alonzo Cushing (G. P. Putnam's Sons, 1906), 355.

CHAPTER 6 | HOW THE BIBLE CAN TRANSFORM KIDS' LIVES

1. George W. Bethune, *Guilt, Grace and Gratitude: Lectures on the Heidelberg Catechism,* 2 vols. (Banner of Truth, 2001).
2. Arnold Cole and Pamela Caudill Ovwigho, *Bible Engagement as the Key to Spiritual Growth: A Research Synthesis* (Center for Bible Engagement, August 2012), 4–5, https://www.centerforbibleengagement.org/_files/ugd/c59c7d_28c00fc7279a44e8832f15503914c426.pdf; see also "Bible Engagement and 'The Power of 4': A Key to Spiritual Growth," Center for Bible Engagement, May 31, 2024, https://www.centerforbibleengagement.org/post/bible-engagement-a-key-to-spiritual-growth.
3. William Jeynes, "The Academic Advantages of the Bible," *First Things*, November 16, 2017, https://www.firstthings.com/web-exclusives/2017/11/the-academic-advantages-of-the-bible.
4. Jeynes, "Academic Advantages of the Bible."
5. "The Bill of Rights: A Transcription," America's Founding Documents, National Archives, last reviewed August 7, 2025, https://www.archives.gov/founding-docs/bill-of-rights-transcript.

6. Supreme Court ruling in Engel v. Vitale (1962), cited in "Religion in the Public Schools," Pew Research Center, October 3, 2019, https://www.pewresearch.org/religion/2019/10/03/religion-in-the-public-schools-2019-update.
7. School District of Abington Township, Pennsylvania v. Schempp, 374 U.S. 203 (1963), case summary, Oyez, https://www.oyez.org/cases/1962/142.
8. Santa Fe Independent School District v. Doe, 530 U.S. 290 (2000), case summary, Oyez, https://www.oyez.org/cases/1999/99-62.

CHAPTER 7 | BEFORE- AND AFTER-SCHOOL BIBLE CLUBS

1. David Kinnaman, "Rising Spiritual Openness in America," Barna, January 18, 2023, https://www.barna.com/research/rising-spiritual-openness. Barna survey was conducted October 21–31, 2022.
2. Kinnaman, "Rising Spiritual Openness in America."
3. Kinnaman, "Rising Spiritual Openness in America."
4. US Department of Education, Schools and the State (ERIC Document ED441724), defining a limited open forum as arising when one or more noncurriculum-related student groups meet during noninstructional time and distinguishing them from curriculum-related groups.
5. Child Evangelism Fellowship, "Our History," accessed August 19, 2025, https://www.cefonline.com/about/history.
6. "Fellowship of Christian Athletes Timeline," FCA, accessed August 19, 2025, https://timeline.fca.org.
7. George Barna, *Raising Spiritual Champions: Nurturing Your Child's Heart, Mind and Soul* (Arizona Christian University Press, 2023), chap. 3.
8. Equal Access Act, H.R. 5345, 98th Cong. (1983–1984), Congress.gov, https://www.congress.gov/bill/98th-congress/house-bill/5345.
9. "U.S. Reports: Westside Community BD. of ED. v. Mergens, 496 U.S. 226 (1990)," Library of Congress, https://www.loc.gov/item/usrep496226. Initially the school board denied the request for a Bible club because the club wouldn't allow a staff member to sponsor it (a requirement of the school at that time). In an 8–1 decision, the Supreme Court upheld the rights of the students to form the Bible club and further ruled that the school providing a staff sponsor would not be an establishment of religion, since the club would be organized by students.
10. "Good News Club," Child Evangelism Fellowship Maryland, accessed August 19, 2025, https://cefmaryland.org/ministries/good-news-club.
11. "Cultivating Character and Reaching KiDs for Christ!," KiDs Beach Club, accessed August 19, 2025, https://www.kidsbeachclub.org.
12. "University of Arizona Conducts Study on the Educational Value of

KiDs Beach Club," KiDs Beach Club, January 23, 2025, https://www.kidsbeachclub.org/blog/university-of-arizona-releases-a-study-on-the-educational-value-of-kids-beach-club.

CHAPTER 8 | BIBLE-LITERACY CLASSES

1. Ken Ham, "The Truth About Our Worldview," episode 128, interview by Kori Pennypacker, *The Bible2School Podcast with Meredith*, February 13, 2024, https://www.bible2school.com/podcast/the-truth-about-our-worldview.
2. Tacitus, *The Annals of Tacitus, Books XI–XVI: An English Translation*, trans. George Gilbert Ramsay, book 15, chap. 44 (John Murray, 1909), 281.
3. Sarah Grace Shewbert, "The Bible's Influence in American Music," *Washington Times*, December 12, 2014, https://www.washingtontimes.com/news/2014/dec/12/bibles-influence-american-music.
4. "Taylor Swift Mocks Christianity in Her New Album," Movieguide, April 23, 2024, https://www.movieguide.org/news-articles/taylor-swift-mocks-christianity-in-her-new-album.html.
5. Kurt Bergdolt, "The Bible's Influence: Influence of the Bible in Art," *Washington Times*, December 11, 2014, https://www.washingtontimes.com/news/2014/dec/11/the-bibles-influence-influence-of-the-bible-in-art.
6. American Bible Society, *State of the Bible USA 2024*, (American Bible Society, 2024), https://www.americanbible.org/wp-content/uploads/2024/12/SOTB-2024-12-Final-1.pdf.
7. American Bible Society, *State of the Bible USA 2025* (American Bible Society, 2025), 20, https://www.americanbible.org/wp-content/uploads/2025/04/SOTB-2025-04-Final.pdf.
8. "Bible in Education," Dunham Bible Museum, Houston Christian University, accessed August 20, 2025, https://hc.edu/museums/dunham-bible-museum/tour-of-the-museum/bible-in-america/bible-in-education.
9. "Teach the Bible in Schools—Academically," Bible Literacy Project, accessed August 20, 2025, https://www.bibleliteracy.org.
10. "It's Coming Back . . . and It's Our Constitutional Right!," National Council on Bible Curriculum in Public Schools, accessed August 20, 2025, https://www.bibleinschools.net.
11. "The Bible's Literature and Legacy *Online*," BibLit, accessed August 20, 2025, https://biblit.org.
12. "About BibLit," BibLit, accessed August 20, 2025, https://biblit.org/about.
13. "The Bill of Rights: A Transcription," America's Founding Documents, National Archives, last reviewed August 7, 2025, https://www.archives.gov/founding-docs/bill-of-rights-transcript.

14. "Guidance on Constitutionally Protected Prayer and Religious Expression in Public Elementary and Secondary Schools," US Department of Education, last reviewed January 14, 2025, https://www2.ed.gov/policy/gen/guid/religionandschools/prayer-guidance-2020.html. Italics in the original.
15. Evie Blad, "Should the Bible Be Taught in Public Schools?," *Education Week*, July 15, 2024, https://www.edweek.org/teaching-learning/should-the-bible-be-taught-in-public-schools/2024/07.
16. "Academic Bible Study Is Legal in the U.S.," Bible Literacy Project, accessed August 21, 2025, https://www.bibleliteracy.org/united-states.
17. "About Us," National Council on Bible Curriculum in Public Schools, accessed August 21, 2025, https://www.bibleinschools.net/About-Us.
18. "About BibLit," https://biblit.org/about.
19. John Farquhar Plake, quoted in Diana Chandler, "State of the Bible: Americans Less Engaged, but Gen Z Bucks Trend," Religion Unplugged, April 18, 2024, https://religionunplugged.com/news/2024/4/17/state-of-the-bible-americans-less-engaged-but-gen-z-bucking-trend.

CHAPTER 9 | RELEASED-TIME BIBLE PROGRAMS

1. "Released Time History," Released Time Religious Education, accessed August 21, 2025, https://www.releasedtime.org/history.
2. Illinois ex rel. McCollum v. Board of Education of School Dist. No. 71, Champaign County, 333 U.S. 203 (1948), case summary, Oyez, https://www.oyez.org/cases/1940-1955/333us203.
3. Zorach v. Clauson, 343 U.S. 306 (1952), case summary, Justia U.S. Supreme Court Center, accessed August 21, 2025, https://supreme.justia.com/cases/federal/us/343/306.
4. "The Bible2School Curriculum," Bible2School, accessed September 24, 2025, https://www.bible2school.com/about-bible2school/the-bible2school-curriculum.
5. "What We Believe," Bible2School, accessed September 24, 2025, https://www.bible2school.com/about-bible2school/what-we-believe.
6. "Why This Matters," Bible2School, accessed August 21, 2025, https://www.bible2school.com/about-bible2school/why-this-matters.
7. "LifeWise Academy 2024 Educators Survey," LifeWise Academy, accessed August 21, 2025, https://lifewise.org/wp-content/uploads/2024/07/Survey-Results.pdf.
8. "Why This Matters," Bible2School.
9. "Why This Matters," Bible2School.
10. "Why Are Released Time Programs on the Rise?," Bible2School,

January 7, 2025, https://www.bible2school.com/blog/why-are-released-time-programs-on-the-rise.

11. LifeWise Academy, *LifeWise Academy Outcomes Report* (TPMA/Ambassador Enterprises, 2023), 3, https://lifewise.org/wp-content/uploads/2024/03/LifeWise-Outcomes-Report-2023-2.pdf.
12. Joel Penton, personal email to author, July 26, 2024.
13. Trace W. Hansen, "The Effect of Daily Released-Time Religious Education on Academic Achievement" master's thesis (Utah State University, 2013), v, https://digitalcommons.usu.edu/cgi/viewcontent.cgi?referer=&httpsredir=1&article=2447&context=etd.

CHAPTER 10 | PREPARING VERSUS PROTECTING

1. Katherine Schaeffer, "U.S. Public, Private and Charter Schools in 5 Charts," Pew Research Center, June 6, 2024, https://www.pewresearch.org/short-reads/2024/06/06/us-public-private-and-charter-schools-in-5-charts.
2. Kori Pennypacker, "Not How We Protect Our Kids from the World, It's How We Prepare Them to Be a Light in the World," *Washington Times*, September 28, 2023, https://www.washingtontimes.com/news/2023/sep/28/not-how-we-protect-our-kids-world-its-how-prepare-.
3. *Merriam-Webster Dictionary*, "atheism," accessed August 22, 2025, https://www.merriam-webster.com/dictionary/atheism.
4. Francis A. Schaeffer, *A Christian Manifesto* (Crossway, 1981), 23.
5. William Temple, quoted in Gordon L. Heath and Steven M. Studebaker, eds., *The Globalization of Christianity: Implications for Christian Ministry and Theology* (Pickwick Publications, 2014), 5.
6. Carl Sagan, *Cosmos* (Ballantine Books, 2013), 1.
7. American Humanist Association and Jason Michael Holden v. United States of America, case no. 3:14-cv-00565-HZ, 63 F.Supp.3d 1274 (D. Or. 2014), https://case-law.vlex.com/vid/am-humanist-ass-n-891177485. See also "Federal Court Rules 'Secular Humanism' a Religion, Extends Equal Protection Rights to Atheists," Christian News Network, November 4, 2014, https://christiannews.net/2014/11/04/federal-court-rules-secular-humanism-a-religion-extends-equal-protection-rights-to-atheists.
8. "Amsterdam Declaration 1952," Policies, Humanists International, World Humanist Congress, Amsterdam, Netherlands, 1952, https://humanists.international/policy/amsterdam-declaration-1952.
9. Abraham Lincoln, *The Collected Works of Abraham Lincoln*, vol. 7, ed. Roy P. Basler (Rutgers University Press, 1953), 542.

10. "Jessica's Daily Self-Affirmations!," Architects of Life, October 20, 2014, YouTube, 49 sec., https://www.youtube.com/watch?v=gIwLciAKe9s.
11. "New Data on Gen Z—Perceptions of Pressure, Anxiety and Empowerment," Barna, January 28, 2021, https://www.barna.com/research/gen-z-success. Barna Group survey of US teens and young adults ages 13–21, conducted between June 15 and July 17, 2020.
12. Hudson Taylor, quoted in *101 Quotable Christians: More Than 2,000 Memorable Thoughts from People Who Shaped Your Faith* (Barbour, 2014), 1993.

CHAPTER 11 | PLAYING ON THE SAME TEAM

1. Kate Anderson, "What Are Parental Rights?," Alliance Defending Freedom, April 28, 2022, https://adflegal.org/article/what-are-parental-rights.

CHAPTER 12 | KINDLY EDUCATING THE EDUCATORS

1. John Wooden and Jay Carty, *Coach Wooden's Pyramid of Success: Building Blocks for a Better Life* (Revell, 2005), 42. This is a cooperation building block of John Wooden's "Pyramid of Success."

CHAPTER 13 | CONVERSATION TOOLS FOR KIDS

1. "Kids Say the Darndest Things," created by Art Linkletter, segment on *House Party*, radio show, first aired on CBS Radio in 1945.

CHAPTER 14 | ROLE MODELS ON SPEED DIAL

1. George Barna, "Release #3: A Detailed Look at How the Worldview of Parents of Preteens Misses the Mark," *American Worldview Inventory 2022*, Cultural Research Center, Arizona Christian University, April 12, 2022, https://www.arizonachristian.edu/wp-content/uploads/2022/04/AWVI2022_Release_03_DigitalVersion.pdf. Also see "American Parents Lack Biblical Worldview, Robust Faith to Share with Kids," Arizona Christian University, March 8, 2022, https://www.arizonachristian.edu/2022/03/08/american-parents-lack-biblical-worldview-robust-faith-to-share-with-kids.
2. Soyiba Jawed et al., "Classification of Visual and Non-visual Learners Using Electroencephalographic Alpha and Gamma Activities," *Frontiers in Behavioral Neuroscience* 13 (May 7, 2019): 86, https://doi.org/10.3389/fnbeh.2019.00086.
3. "Visual Learning Style: Key Characteristics and Benefits," Crawford International, May 17, 2024, https://www.crawfordinternational.co.za/blog/the-visual-learning-style.

4. Kara E. Powell and Chap Clark, *Sticky Faith: Everyday Ideas to Build Lasting Faith in Your Kids* (Zondervan, 2011).
5. Powell and Clark, *Sticky Faith*, chap. 5.
6. Joseph P. Tierney et al., *Making a Difference: An Impact Study of Big Brothers Big Sisters* (Public/Private Ventures, 1995), 20, 30.
7. "Who Mentored You?," Mentor, accessed December 30, 2025, https://www.mentoring.org/resource/who-mentored-you.
8. "Roger and Kli Kli Story," Bible2School, September 9, 2024, YouTube, 2 min., 59 sec., https://www.youtube.com/watch?v=qYOf7UTXoVA.

CHAPTER 15 | IT'S TIME TO GET IN THE GAME!

1. Jasper Tjaden et al., "The Long-Term Effects of Time Use During High School on Positive Development," *Longitudinal and Life Course Studies* 10, no. 1 (2019): table 3, https://www.ncbi.nlm.nih.gov/pmc/articles/PMC6720124.
2. Stephen R. Covey, *The Seven Habits of Highly Effective People: Powerful Lessons in Personal Change* (Free Press, 2004), 161.

ABOUT THE AUTHOR

Kori Pennypacker is on a mission to help redefine how America thinks about religion during the public-school day. She serves as the CEO of Bible2School, a public-school ministry, where she oversees the mission and builds relationships with businesses, churches, and community leaders on the topic of the importance of spiritual training for children nationwide. Kori loves inviting people into the Bible2School team as valued members, volunteers, and donors.

Kori has a bachelor's degree from Shippensburg University and more than twenty-five years of experience in children's ministry and leadership. Her passion and enthusiasm for Jesus and children have led her to various speaking engagements, such as conferences, TV appearances, radio shows, and podcasts. She has been a guest of Focus on the Family, CBN, *Dr. James Dobson's Family Talk*, Truth & Liberty, the Association for Biblical Higher Education (ABHE), *Morning Light Live*, the Creation Museum, Bott Radio Network, Family Life Radio, Faith Radio, Moms in Prayer, iWork4Him, *Joe Watkins: State of Independence*, the *Tremendous Leadership* podcast, *WISE and Otherwise*, and *Zero Compromise*. She has also been a monthly contributor to *The Washington Times*'s Higher Ground.

In addition, Kori hosts inspirational webinars, such as "God Was *Not* Taken out of Public Schools," a thirty-five-minute recording in which she discusses how children can legally bring their faith into public school.

In her spare time, Kori can be found whipping up a Crock-Pot meal for her family for game night, enjoying God's creation on biking trails, babysitting her grandchildren, and volunteering alongside her husband to mentor engaged couples in their local church.

IT'S OFFICIAL:

Parenting Gen Z is super hard.

Gen Z is the most non-Christian generation in our history.

The culture is shifting faster than parents can keep up and any false step can shut the door on faith talks. This book will help you guide your Gen Z child through a bunch of topics, including:

Why faith?
Gaming limits
Depression
LGBQTIA
Sex/Porn

Order your copy!
Store.FocusOnTheFamily.com

FOCUS ON THE FAMILY.

DOT 348362